MW00397076

Cooking Wild Game & Fish Southern Style

Pete, Good luck to you as you pursue your dreams elsewhere! I hope you will truly be happy in your future endeavors. We have enjoyed having you here with us this year at KCHS. Good luck! Carol Jarvis

Coach Dewease,
Best of luck in Florida! You will be missed here at KCHS! Thanks for the friendship, the positive attitude, and the willingness to help students and faculty. From a State fan to an Ole Miss fan... "Go to Hell Ole Miss!"
Love
Sheila Aust

Best Wishes,
[illegible]
LTC, USA (RET)

Best Wishes for a great year in Florida + Remember Mississippi is still on the Map! Miss you!
Barbara Breckenridge

Cooking Wild Game & Fish Southern Style

Billy Joe Cross

Cooking Wild Game & Fish
Southern Style

#3 Le Bourgeois
Brandon, Mississippi 39047

This book is a collection of our favorite recipes, which are not necessarily original recipes. The recipes in this book have been collected from various sources, and neither Billy Joe Cross nor any contributor, publisher, printer, distributor, or seller of this book is responsible for errors or omissions.

Library of Congress Number: 00-090335
ISBN: 0-9677762-0-1

Designed, Edited, and Manufactured by
Favorite Recipes® Press
An imprint of

FRP™

P.O. Box 305142
Nashville, Tennessee 37230
1-800-358-0560

Book Design and Art Direction: Steve Newman
Project Manager: Nicki Pendleton Wood

Manufactured in the United States of America
First Edition 1976
Fourth Edition 2000 10,000 copies

Dedication

To those who measure their sporting pleasure not by the weight of the game bag, but by the richness of the experience, this book is dedicated.
May you live in rhythm with the seasons,
know the tired contentment of long days afield,
and do so always in the company of very good friends.

And to my darling wife, Robbie, a true helpmate in preparing this new edition. It is dedicated to you because it could not have happened without you.

The Cover Art

"Southern Morning, Wild Turkey" by R. J. McDonald
Countryside Studios, 1-800-235-1402

The Photographs

Chapters 1–4, Joe Mac Hudspeth Jr.
1-601-992-0752

Preface

As every hunter knows, cooking wild game is as exciting and gratifying as hunting it. After a day spent outdoors, appetites are strong, and centuries of evolution fall away as we enjoy the harvest of this ancient sport. The tantalizing aroma is made all the more enticing by the richness that simply cannot be matched at the local deli.

Since hunters are also innately adventurous, we are always in pursuit of new and ever more delectable ways of preparing the day's take. The recipes in this book offer a veritable smorgasbord of everything from the savory main course to serve-alongs such as soups and desserts. I think it is safe to say that hunters and fishermen are some of the best cooks in the world! You'll find dishes to please the most discriminating of tastes and enough variety to pique your interest throughout the seasons. This is the kind of authentic, down-home food that satisfies the taste buds and soothes the soul.

As you turn the pages of this book, I predict that you will begin to notice a hollow feeling in the pit of your stomach, and you will suddenly realize how hungry you are. Just browsing through the recipes will make you want to go straight to your freezer and take out that carefully wrapped package you've been saving for just the right recipe. Wild game is a precious commodity that deserves the utmost care in preparation and the perfect blend of seasoning. These recipes will guide you, in an easy-to-read format, from the preparations to setting your dish on the table. The recipes come from many of the best cooks in the South, but the accolades from friends and loved ones will be yours.

Enjoy.

Billy Joe Cross

Table of Contents

Big Game

Big Game

Big Game
Big Game
Big Game
Big Game
Big Game
Big Game
Big Game

Roast Leg of Venison

1 leg of venison
4 garlic cloves, sliced
1 pound salt pork, sliced
Salt and pepper to taste
1 cup flour
1 cup bacon drippings, melted

Refrigerate the venison for 1 or 2 days before cooking. Place the meat in a large roasting pan. Pierce holes in the meat with a small knife and insert garlic. Lay strips of salt pork over meat. Sprinkle with salt, pepper and flour. Pour the bacon drippings over meat. Bake in a 350-degree oven for 20 to 25 minutes per pound, basting often with pan juices. Makes 8 servings.

Venison Care

Venison is delicious when properly processed in the field. High hunting season temperatures in the South mean extra care must be taken to dress and cool the animal as quickly as possible. When processing, be careful not to get either foreign matter or urine on the meat. Remove any excess blood from the body cavity and cut out damaged areas of tissue.

The body cavity should be propped open to allow air to circulate and dissipate body heat. The animal should be kept cool while transporting. This means not transporting it on the hood of a vehicle nor in the trunk of a vehicle. A rack on the roof or in the bed of a truck is an ideal place. Always cover the animal with canvas or plastic.

Proper aging adds to the texture of the meat. To age, hang the skinned animal in a cooler for 10 to 12 days at a temperature of 35 to 40 degrees F. You may quarter the animal and place the quarters on wire racks in a refrigerator for the same length of time.

When the meat has aged, the hunter can take a sharp fillet knife and remove all muscles from the leg bones. He should follow the lines between each muscle to separate them, then remove everything white from these muscles: sinew, ligaments, tendons, cartilage, and fat. Wrap each muscle in plastic wrap and squeeze all air from the wrap. Then wrap in heavy-duty aluminum foil and secure with tape. Identify each piece with its name on a piece of freezer tape affixed to the package: od (old doe) from hq (from hindquarters). Then add the date. Other useful abbreviations include: ob (old buck); yd (young doe); yb (young buck).

Smoked Venison

1 hindquarter venison
Garlic salt to taste
1 pound bacon

To prepare the venison, separate each individual muscle and remove from hindquarter. Remove all fat, tendons, ligaments and sheaths. Sprinkle the meat liberally with garlic salt.

Fry 6 strips of bacon in a skillet. Set the bacon aside for another use. Brush slightly cooled drippings over meat. Place an uncooked slice of bacon on each piece of meat. Smoke in a prepared smoker over hickory chips for 1 1/4 hours, maintaining a temperature of 190 to 200 degrees, until largest pieces cook to medium-rare. Slice thinly. Makes 8 servings.

Red Wine Venison Roast

1 (4- to 5-pound) venison roast, trimmed
3/4 cup beef suet
1/2 teaspoon salt
1/4 teaspoon pepper
3 small garlic cloves, sliced
1 1/4 cups red burgundy

Rub the venison on all sides with the beef suet, salt and pepper. Make small slits on all sides of the meat and insert the garlic. Bake in an open pan at 325 degrees for about 2 1/2 hours. Pour wine over roast during the last hour of cooking. Baste frequently with pan juices during the last hour. Makes 10 servings.

On-the-Grill Venison Pot Roast

1 (4- to 5-pound) venison roast
1 pound bacon
3 garlic cloves, sliced
2 medium onions, quartered
4 medium potatoes, quartered
3 ribs celery, sliced
4 large carrots, cut into chunks
3 tablespoons soy sauce
3 tablespoons Worcestershire sauce

Make 8 large slits all the way through the roast with a large knife. Push some of the bacon and and all of the garlic into the holes. Wrap bacon around roast and secure with wooden picks. Place roast, onions, potatoes, celery, carrots, soy sauce and Worcestershire sauce in heavy-duty aluminum foil and wrap securely. Place the foil-wrapped roast in a covered pan. Place on a grill rack and grill over low flame for about 2 hours. Makes 10 to 12 servings.

Buttery Pot Roast

1 (3- to 5-pound) venison roast
1/2 cup Worcestershire sauce
2 tablespoons soy sauce
1 tablespoon salt
1 cup (2 sticks) butter
1 cup water
2 cups wine, beer or cola
1 teaspoon lemon juice
Pepper to taste

Place the roast in a large glass dish. Combine the Worcestershire sauce, soy sauce, salt, butter, water, wine, lemon juice and pepper in a bowl and pour over the roast. Refrigerate, covered, for several hours. Drain and discard liquid. Place the meat in a large covered roasting pan. Bake at 300 degrees for 4 hours. If you like, add chopped onions, potatoes, carrots and/or sweet potatoes about 30 minutes before the end of the cooking process.
Makes 8 to 10 servings.

Texas-Style Pot-Roasted Venison

1 (4-pound) venison roast
3 tablespoons peanut oil
6 garlic cloves, sliced
1 envelope onion soup mix
12 ounces cola

Score the roast in several places. Rub the peanut oil over roast. Poke holes in roast with a small knife and insert the garlic. Spread the soup mix over the roast. Place a large sheet of aluminum foil in a roasting pan. Place the roast on the foil. Pour cola around the roast. Seal foil tightly. Bake at 300 degrees for 3 hours. Makes 6 to 8 servings.

Easy Oven-Bag Dinner

$1/2$ cup red wine
1 tablespoon flour
1 (3- to 4-pound) venison roast, cut 4 inches thick
Salt and pepper to taste
1 medium onion, cut into quarters
2 bay leaves

Combine the wine and flour in a small bowl and mix until smooth. Pour into an oven bag. Rub the roast with salt and pepper. Place the roast in the bag. Add onion to bag. Break bay leaves and add to bag. Seal bag. Cut slits in the top according to package directions. Place the bag in a baking dish. Bake at 325 degrees for 2 to $2\frac{1}{2}$ hours or until meat is cooked through. Discard bay leaves before serving. Makes 8 servings.

Foil-Roasted Venison

1 (3- to 4-pound) venison roast
$1/2$ envelope onion soup mix

Place a large sheet of heavy-duty aluminum foil in a roasting pan. Place the roast on the foil. Sprinkle with the onion soup mix. Bring the edges of foil together and seal tightly. Bake at 300 degrees for $2\frac{1}{2}$ hours. There will be plenty of pan juices collected in the foil. If you like, use these to make gravy. Makes 6 to 8 servings.

Slow-Cooker Roast

1 (2- to 4-pound) venison roast
Salt and pepper to taste
1 cup flour
1/2 cup peanut oil
1 (16-ounce) can whole tomatoes
2 tablespoons brown sugar
1 teaspoon dry mustard
1/4 cup lemon juice
2 garlic cloves
1 onion, chopped
1 tablespoon Worcestershire sauce
1 cup water

Season the roast with salt and pepper. Roll in flour to coat. Brown the roast in peanut oil in a large skillet over medium-high heat. Place roast with tomatoes, brown sugar, dry mustard, lemon juice, garlic, onion, Worcestershire sauce and water in a slow cooker. Cook on high for 2 hours. Turn heat to low and cook until meat is tender, about 3 hours longer. You may also cook this roast on low for 8 hours. Makes 6 servings.

Marinade for Venison

2 cups wine vinegar or other vinegar
2 tablespoons sugar
2 cups water
1/2 teaspoon whole peppercorns
2 carrots, sliced
3 onions, sliced
12 whole cloves
1 teaspoon mustard seeds
2 teaspoons salt
4 bay leaves

Combine the wine vinegar, sugar, water, peppercorns, carrots, onions, cloves, mustard seeds, salt and bay leaves in a large plastic food bag or bowl. Add up to 10 pounds venison and marinate in the refrigerator for 48 to 72 hours. The meat will be tenderized, flavored and ready to pot-roast or oven-roast. Remove bay leaves before serving. Makes enough marinade for 10 pounds of meat.

Fruit and Sausage Shoulder Roast

2 to 4 pounds venison shoulder
2 large white onions, sliced
2 pounds smoked link sausage, thinly sliced on the diagonal
2 large green apples, sliced
Garlic salt and lemon pepper to taste
1 cup (2 sticks) margarine
1 fresh pineapple, peeled, cored, sliced

Cut a long slit in the venison along the shoulder bone. Insert about a quarter of the onion slices into the slit. Insert some of the sausage slices into the slit with the onions.

Place a large piece of heavy-duty aluminum foil into a roasting pan, leaving enough overlap to fold over roast. Arrange apples and remaining onions on foil. Place the roast on top of the apples and onions.

Season the roast with garlic salt and lemon pepper. Top with margarine, pineapple slices and remaining sausage. Seal the foil tightly around the roast. Roast at 325 degrees for 3 hours. Serve with hot cooked wild and white rice mixture. Makes 4 to 8 servings.

Cheese-Stuffed Smoked Venison

1 venison backstrap
1 cup teriyaki sauce
1 cup Italian-seasoned bread crumbs
1 cup shredded Swiss cheese
1 cup shredded sharp Cheddar cheese
4 thin slices ham
6 slices bacon

Cut the backstrap lengthwise two-thirds of the way through. Open it like a book. Cover with plastic wrap. Pound with a meat mallet until meat is an even thickness. Remove plastic wrap. Combine the meat with teriyaki sauce in a large glass container. Refrigerate for 30 minutes.

Sprinkle the meat generously with bread crumbs and cheeses, patting lightly so crumbs and cheeses will adhere. Arrange the ham slices over meat. Roll to enclose crumbs, cheese and ham. Wrap the bacon around the meat roll and secure with wooden picks. Smoke the meat in a water smoker over wet chips for 45 minutes or until cooked through. Slice and serve hot. This dish freezes well after cooking, wrapped securely in plastic wrap, then in aluminum foil. Makes 8 to 10 servings.

Rolled Stuffed Roast

1½ cups bread crumbs
2 teaspoons bacon drippings
¼ cup diced onion
¼ cup diced celery
¼ cup diced green bell pepper
1 cup drained canned tomatoes
¼ cup chopped fresh parsley
1 teaspoon dry mustard
1 teaspoon white pepper
Dash curry powder
Dash garlic powder
1 large venison steak, about 1 pound, cut ½ inch thick
6 tablespoons butter, melted
3 tablespoons Worcestershire sauce
3 tablespoons soy sauce
¼ teaspoon salt
Dash garlic powder

Combine the crumbs, bacon drippings, onion, celery, bell pepper, tomatoes, parsley, mustard, pepper, curry powder and garlic powder in a large bowl and mix well. Spread evenly over the steak. Roll to enclose filling and tie with kitchen twine. Place the stuffed steak in a baking dish. Bake at 350 degrees for 1½ hours. Combine butter, Worcestershire sauce, soy sauce, salt and garlic powder in a small bowl and mix well. Brush over roast occasionally during baking. Makes 4 to 6 servings.

Pan-Fried Venison Steak

1 (2-pound) venison "ham" steak, cut 3/4 inch thick
1/2 cup heavy cream or evaporated milk
1/3 cup flour
3 tablespoons butter
Salt and pepper to taste

Pound the steak with a meat mallet to tenderize. Cut into serving pieces. Dip the meat into the cream in a shallow pan, then coat with flour. Brown in hot butter in a large skillet, sprinkling with salt and pepper to taste and turning halfway through the cooking time. Serve hot.
Makes 4 servings.

Deer Steak and Gravy

6 medium venison steaks, cut 1/2 inch thick
1 cup flour
1/2 teaspoon salt
1/2 teaspoon pepper
1 cup vegetable oil
2 large onions, sliced
6 garlic cloves, crushed
4 beef bouillon cubes
1 quart water

Pound the steaks with a meat mallet to tenderize. Combine flour, salt and pepper and coat steaks with mixture. Brown in hot oil in a Dutch oven. Add onions, garlic, bouillon cubes and water to the pot. Bring to a boil; reduce heat. Simmer, uncovered, for 45 minutes or until gravy is thick.
Makes 6 servings.

Tangy Oven-Barbecued Steak

1 cup grape jelly
1/4 cup A.1. steak sauce
2 envelopes onion soup mix
1/2 teaspoon salt
1/3 teaspoon pepper
3 pounds venison steak

Combine the jelly, steak sauce, soup mix, salt and pepper in a large bowl and mix well. Place the steak on foil in a shallow baking pan. Pour three-fourths of the sauce mixture over the steak. Seal foil tightly around steak. Bake in a 350-degree oven for 2 hours or until meat is tender. Open the foil for the final 5 minutes of cooking, basting meat with remaining sauce. Makes 6 to 8 servings.

Slow-Cooker Steaks

2 to 3 pounds venison steaks
1/2 cup flour
1/2 teaspoon salt
1/3 teaspoon pepper
1/3 teaspoon lemon pepper
1 cup vegetable oil
1 (10-ounce) can cream of mushroom soup
1 (10-ounce) can cream of celery soup
1 onion, chopped
10 ounces water
1/2 green bell pepper, chopped

Coat the steaks with the flour combined with salt, pepper and lemon pepper. Brown in hot oil in a large skillet. Remove from skillet and place in a slow cooker. Add soups, onion, water and bell pepper. Cook on low to medium for 4 to 6 hours. Serve over rice.
Makes 6 to 8 servings.

Mustardy Simmered Steaks

4 pounds lean venison "ham" or shoulder
Salt and pepper to taste
$1^1/_2$ cups flour for coating
Vegetable oil
1 medium onion, chopped
6 garlic cloves, chopped
$^3/_4$ cup Worcestershire sauce
$^3/_4$ cup wine vinegar
Pinch of allspice
1 (6-ounce) jar prepared mustard
1 bay leaf

Cut the venison into steaks $^1/_4$ inch thick. Salt and pepper to taste. Coat with the flour. Brown lightly in a small amount of hot oil in a skillet. Combine the onion, garlic, Worcestershire sauce, vinegar, allspice, mustard and bay leaf in a large saucepan. Cook over medium heat until light brown. Place the steaks in a roasting pan or large skillet and pour the sauce over the steaks until it is even with the level of the meat. (Do not cover the steaks with sauce.) Simmer, covered, over low heat for 2 hours or until steaks are tender, stirring occasionally. Remove the bay leaf before serving. Serve with sweet potatoes, a green vegetable and hot biscuits. Makes 8 to 10 servings.

Marinated Venison and Vegetables

2 pounds venison, cubed
1 (16-ounce) bottle Italian salad dressing
2 large onions
2 large green bell peppers
1 pint cherry tomatoes
1 pound bacon
8 ounces mushrooms

Combine the venison and salad dressing in a glass or plastic container. Marinate in the refrigerator for at least 2 hours. Drain, reserving the marinade. Cut the onions and bell peppers into 1-inch chunks. Cut the cherry tomatoes into halves. Cut the bacon into $1^1/_2$-inch lengths. Soak wooden skewers in water to cover for 30 minutes. Alternate the venison, bacon, onions, bell peppers, cherry tomatoes and mushrooms alternately on skewers, making sure to place bacon on either side of venison. Pour the marinade over prepared skewers. Grill or broil, turning occasionally, until meat is cooked to medium-rare. Makes 6 servings.

Italian-Style Venison Skewers

1/2 cup lemon juice
1 cup olive oil
1 1/4 teaspoons oregano, crumbled
3 garlic cloves, minced or put through a press
3 pounds venison loin, cut into chunks
1 pound bacon, cut into 1 1/2-inch lengths
3 large onions, cut into quarters
3 large bell peppers, any color, cut into chunks

Combine the lemon juice, olive oil, oregano and garlic in a heavy-duty sealable plastic bag. Add the venison and shake to coat. Refrigerate for 4 to 6 hours, turning bag every hour. Soak wooden skewers in water to cover for 30 minutes. When ready to cook, drain and discard marinade. Alternate chunks of the venison, bacon, onions and bell peppers on skewers, making sure that bacon is on both sides of each piece of venison. Grill until meat is cooked to medium-rare, turning occasionally. Makes 6 to 8 servings.

Wild Sukiyaki

2 pounds venison tenderloin
12 mushrooms
3 bunches green onions
4 heads broccoli
1 (1-inch) piece deer suet
1 (14-ounce) can mixed Chinese or chop suey vegetables, drained
1 tablespoon plus 1 teaspoon sugar
1/2 cup soy sauce
1 (3-ounce) can chow mein noodles

Cut the venison into paper-thin slices about 2 inches square. (Freezing the meat for 30 minutes makes it easier to cut thin slices.) Thinly slice the mushrooms, green onions and broccoli. Place the deer suet in a skillet and cook over low heat until oil is rendered. Increase heat to medium, add vegetables and cook for several minutes until tender-crisp. Add the meat, mushrooms, sugar and soy sauce. Cook for 10 minutes, stirring constantly. Serve over hot cooked rice topped with French-fried onions and chow mein noodles. Makes 4 to 6 servings.

Camp Stew

2 venison loins, about 8 to 10 pounds total, cut into cubes
1/2 cup flour
Salt and pepper to taste
1/2 cup vegetable oil
3 medium onions, diced
2 cans mushroom stems and pieces
1 cup beef broth or 4 beef bouillon cubes dissolved in 1 cup hot water
3/4 cup dry red wine
1/4 cup ketchup
1 teaspoon Worcestershire sauce
6 carrots, cut diagonally

Coat the venison in flour combined with salt and pepper. Brown in hot oil in a large skillet. Remove from skillet. Cook the onions and mushrooms in skillet until onions are tender. Add the broth, wine, ketchup, Worcestershire sauce and salt and pepper to taste. Simmer for 45 minutes. Add the carrots and simmer for 45 minutes longer. Serve over rice. Makes 16 to 20 servings.

Fruited Venison Stew

2 pounds venison
1 tablespoon butter
1 (15-ounce) can juice-pack pineapple chunks, drained
1 (16-ounce) can whole tomatoes
1 tablespoon Lawry's seasoned salt
1 teaspoon pepper
1/2 teaspoon garlic powder
1 teaspoon oregano
1/2 bay leaf
4 small onions, quartered
1 large sweet potato, sliced
1 large green bell pepper, chopped

Brown the venison in butter in a heavy 2-quart pan. Add the pineapple, undrained tomatoes, seasoned salt, pepper, garlic powder, oregano, bay leaf, onions and sweet potato. Simmer, covered, for 1 1/2 to 2 hours or until tender. Add the bell pepper and cook for 10 minutes. Remove bay leaf before serving. Makes 6 servings.

Venison and Wild Rice Stew

3 to 4 pounds venison
2 large onions, sliced
2 quarts water
2 teaspoons salt
Dash freshly ground pepper
$1^1/2$ cups wild rice, washed

Cut the venison into 2-inch cubes. Combine the venison, onions and water in a large skillet. Bring to a simmer and cook, uncovered, for 3 hours or until venison is tender. Add the salt, pepper and wild rice to skillet and mix well. Simmer, covered, for 20 minutes. Uncover, stir and simmer for 20 minutes longer or until rice is tender and most of the liquid is absorbed. Makes 8 to 10 servings.

Venison Stew with Wine

4 to 5 pounds cubed venison
2 cups flour
$^1/2$ teaspoon Lawry's seasoned salt
$^1/2$ teaspoon white pepper
2 tablespoons bacon drippings
2 onions, diced
1 cup celery, diced
2 beef bouillon cubes
4 cups water
$^1/2$ cup dry red wine
1 (16-ounce) can whole tomatoes
1 (8-ounce) can tomato sauce
1 cup diced potatoes
Dash garlic powder
Dash dry mustard
Dash curry powder

Coat the venison with flour combined with seasoned salt and pepper. Brown in bacon drippings in a large skillet. Add the onions and celery and cook until vegetables are tender. Dissolve bouillon cubes in water mixed with wine in a bowl. Add to the skillet along with tomatoes, tomato sauce, potatoes, garlic powder, dry mustard and curry powder. Cook, covered, over low heat for $2^1/2$ hours. Excellent served over rice. Makes 10 to 12 servings.

Venison Stroganoff

2 pounds venison steaks
1 teaspoon salt
2 tablespoons flour
2 tablespoons butter
2 cups sliced mushrooms
1 cup chopped onions
2 garlic cloves, minced
3 tablespoons flour
2 tablespoons tomato paste
2 cups cold beef stock
3 tablespoons cooking sherry
2 cups sour cream

Cut the venison into 1/4-inch strips. Sprinkle with salt and coat with 2 tablespoons flour. Heat a heavy skillet over medium heat. Add the butter and heat until melted. Sear meat quickly, turning to cook all sides. Remove from skillet. Add the mushrooms, onions and garlic to skillet. Cook for 3 to 4 minutes or until onions are barely tender, stirring constantly. Add 3 tablespoons flour to the skillet and mix well. Add tomato paste and beef stock and mix well. Return meat to skillet. Stir in the sherry and sour cream and heat briefly. Serve with rice or noodles. Makes 4 to 6 servings.

Mississippi Chunky Chili

3 pounds venison stew meat, cut into bite-size pieces
3 tablespoons vegetable oil
3 green bell peppers, diced
2 medium onions, diced
1/2 cup diced celery
2 tablespoons bacon drippings
1 (16-ounce) can tomatoes
2 tablespoons chili powder
1 teaspoon pepper
1 cup water
1/2 teaspoon garlic powder
2 tablespoons parsley flakes
1 teaspoon salt
3 tablespoons ground cumin
3 (16-ounce) cans red kidney beans, drained

Brown the venison in hot oil in a pan. Sauté the bell peppers, onions and celery in bacon drippings in a skillet. Add the vegetables to meat. Add the tomatoes, chili powder, pepper, water, garlic powder, parsley, salt and cumin and mix well. Cook, covered, over low heat for 1 1/2 hours. Add the beans and cook for 20 minutes longer. Makes 8 to 10 servings.

Slow-Simmered Venison Chili

2 pounds ground venison
3 tablespoons vegetable oil
2 (16-ounce) cans kidney beans
2 (8-ounce) cans tomato sauce
3 tablespoons chili powder
1/2 teaspoon cayenne pepper, or to taste
1/2 teaspoon garlic powder
1/2 teaspoon oregano
1/2 teaspoon salt
2 teaspoons ground cumin
1/2 cup minced dried onions
1 cup water

Brown the venison in hot oil in a medium pot. Add the kidney beans, tomato sauce, chili powder, cayenne, garlic powder, oregano, salt, cumin, onions and water and mix well. Simmer for 1 1/2 hours, stirring occasionally. Add additional water if chili is too thick. Makes 6 servings.

Thirty-Minute Deer Chili

2 pounds ground venison
1/4 cup vegetable oil
2 large onions, chopped
3 garlic cloves, chopped
2 bell peppers, chopped
1/4 cup chili powder
1 1/2 teaspoons mild paprika
1 teaspoon Lawry's seasoned salt
1 (16-ounce) can tomatoes
4 cups water
1 (16-ounce) can kidney beans
2 tablespoons ground cumin
Salt and pepper to taste

Brown the venison in hot oil in a large saucepan. Add the onions, garlic and bell peppers and sauté until tender. Add chili powder, paprika, seasoned salt, tomatoes, water, beans, cumin, salt and pepper and mix well. Simmer for 30 minutes. Makes 6 servings.

Venison Hot Tamales

3 pounds venison backstrap
1 pound pork tenderloin
6 garlic cloves
2 teaspoons salt
2 teaspoons dried cilantro
65 dried cornhusks
6 large dried red chiles
2 teaspoons shortening
1 1/2 teaspoons flour
1 teaspoon ground cumin
1 teaspoon salt
1/4 teaspoon baking soda
3 cups corn flour (masa harina)
1 teaspoon salt
5 tablespoons shortening
Venison Tamale Sauce

Place the venison and pork in 2 separate stockpots and cover with water. Add 4 garlic cloves to the stockpot with the venison; add 2 garlic cloves to the stockpot with the pork. Add 1 teaspoon salt and 1 teaspoon cilantro to each stockpot. Bring water in the stockpots to a boil over medium heat. Simmer for 3 hours or until meat is very tender. Drain, reserving venison stock. Shred meats in a food processor or with a fork.

Pour boiling water over about 65 cornhusks in a large bowl. Drain. Cover with more boiling water. Let stand for several hours.

Discard seeds from the dried chiles. Bring chiles and water to cover to a boil in a saucepan over medium heat. Simmer for 30 minutes. Drain, reserving liquid. Let chiles cool in a paper bag. Peel off skins. Combine pulp and 1 cup cooking liquid in a blender or food processor. Process until smooth.

Melt 2 teaspoons shortening in a small saucepan. Add flour and cumin, stirring until well blended. Remove from heat. Stir in half the puréed chile mixture and 1 teaspoon salt. Add to shredded meats and mix well.

Bring the reserved venison stock to a boil in a saucepan. Combine corn flour, 1 teaspoon salt, baking soda and 5 tablespoons shortening in a bowl, stirring until well mixed. Stir in 1 1/4 cups hot stock to make a stiff dough. Stir in remaining chile mixture.

To Assemble the Venison Hot Tamales

Drain the cornhusks and pat dry. Place about 3 tablespoons masa dough in the center of each cornhusk. Spread the dough to within 1/2 inch of edge. Place 2 to 3 tablespoons meat mixture in center. Bring the long sides of husk toward center, enclosing the meat mixture with masa dough. Press the dough gently to seal around meat filling.

Wrap the cornhusk around the masa dough, folding each end under neatly. Use another husk to wrap each tamale again. Tie at each end with a 1/4-inch-wide strip of cornhusk cut from the 5 remaining cornhusks.

Bring a few inches of water to a boil in a deep pan or steamer. Place a steamer rack above the water level. Arrange the tamales on the rack. Cover the pan. Steam the tamales over low heat for about 1 hour or until masa is firm and pulls away from the cornhusks. Serve with Venison Tamale Sauce. Garnish with cilantro.

Makes 30 tamales.

Venison Tamale Sauce

1 (10-ounce) can beef consommé
1/2 cup (1 stick) unsalted butter, melted
1/2 cup flour
6 garlic cloves, minced
2 (8-ounce) cans tomato sauce
2 tablespoons chili powder
2 teaspoons sage
1 teaspoon ground cumin
1/2 teaspoon prepared mole paste
1/2 pound ground venison, browned and drained

Add enough water to the consommé to measure 2 cups. Combine with the butter, flour, garlic, tomato sauce, chili powder, sage and cumin in a saucepan and mix well. Add the mole paste and mix well. Add the ground venison and remove from heat. Serve over tamales. Makes about 6 cups.

Venison Chop Suey

1 pound venison, cut into cubes
1/4 cup (1/2 stick) butter or margarine
1 cup chopped onions
2 cups chopped celery
2 tablespoons molasses
2 tablespoons soy sauce
1 (14-ounce) can bean sprouts
3 tablespoons cornstarch

Sauté the venison in butter in a skillet, but do not brown. Add the onions, celery, molasses and soy sauce and cook for 5 minutes or until onions are tender-crisp. Drain the bean sprouts, reserving liquid. Combine the liquid with cornstarch in a small bowl. Pour over the meat and vegetables in skillet and cook until thickened, stirring constantly. Add the bean sprouts and cook until heated through. Serve over rice or chow mein noodles if desired. Makes 4 to 6 servings.

Sweet-and-Sour Spareribs

3 pounds venison spareribs
2 cups water
1/4 cup soy sauce
Salt to taste
3 tablespoons vinegar
3 tablespoons sugar
2 tablespoons cornstarch
1/2 cup water

Cut the ribs crosswise into short pieces. Place the ribs, 2 cups water, soy sauce and salt in a pan. Bring to a boil, reduce heat and simmer, covered, for 1 hour. Remove ribs from boiling liquid and place in a large skillet, reserving the cooking liquid. Combine the vinegar, sugar, cornstarch, 1/2 cup water and reserved cooking liquid in a pan and mix well. Cook over low heat until mixture is thickened. Pour over the ribs and cook for a few minutes until glazed and tender. Makes 4 to 6 servings.

Spicy Venison Party Dip

1 pound ground venison
2 tablespoons olive oil
2 pounds process American cheese, cut into pieces
1 (10-ounce) can diced tomatoes with green chiles

Brown the venison in olive oil in a skillet; drain. Place the meat, cheese and tomatoes in a slow cooker. Cook, covered, on low until cheese is melted. Serve with tortilla chips. Makes 25 to 30 servings.

Venison-Stuffed Bell Peppers

7 large bell peppers, cut into halves crosswise and cored
2 1/2 pounds ground venison
2 tablespoons vegetable oil
1 bunch green onions, finely chopped
1 1/2 large onions, finely chopped
1/3 cup finely chopped celery
1/2 cup finely chopped bell pepper
1/2 teaspoon garlic powder
1/2 loaf dry bread
2 cups milk
Salt and pepper to taste
1/2 cup bread crumbs

Bring the bell pepper halves and water to cover to a boil in a large pan. Boil for 5 minutes, drain and cover with cold water to stop cooking.

Brown the venison in oil in a large skillet with the green onions, onions, celery, 1/2 cup bell pepper and garlic powder. Cook until onions are tender. Combine the bread and milk in a large bowl and let stand to soften. Add softened bread, salt and pepper to venison. (You may need additional milk.) Stuff bread mixture into parboiled peppers. Arrange in a baking dish. Top with bread crumbs. Bake at 350 degrees for about 30 minutes. Makes 14 servings.

Tangy Two-Meat Loaf

2 pounds ground venison
$1/4$ pound pork sausage
2 teaspoons butter
2 eggs
2 onions, finely chopped
2 ribs celery, chopped
1 cup dry bread crumbs
$1/4$ cup chili sauce
$1/2$ teaspoon thyme
$1/4$ cup dry red wine
1 (8-ounce) can tomato paste
Salt and pepper to taste

Combine the venison and sausage in a large bowl and mix thoroughly. Add the butter, eggs, onions, celery, bread crumbs, chili sauce, thyme, wine and tomato paste and mix well. Season with salt and pepper. Form the mixture into a loaf in a buttered baking dish. Bake at 400 degrees for $1\frac{1}{4}$ hours. Makes 6 servings.

Wild Meat Loaf

1 medium onion, chopped
1 teaspoon margarine
2 pounds ground venison
2 eggs
1 cup water
$1/2$ cup ketchup
$1\frac{3}{4}$ cups soft bread crumbs
1 envelope onion soup mix

Sauté the onion in margarine in a small skillet. Combine the onion, venison, eggs, water, ketchup, bread crumbs and soup mix in a large bowl and mix well. Shape into a loaf in a large baking dish. Bake at 350 degrees for 1 hour. Makes 6 servings.

Delta Venison Meat Loaf

- 2 pounds ground venison
- 1 cup crumbled cooked bacon
- 1 cup bread crumbs
- 1 cup diced green bell pepper
- 1/2 teaspoon white pepper
- 1 teaspoon dry mustard
- 1 tablespoon Worcestershire sauce
- 1/4 teaspoon garlic powder
- 1/4 teaspoon curry powder
- 1/2 teaspoon Chowchow (page 150) or pepper relish
- 1/4 cup chopped canned tomatoes
- 2 eggs
- 1 large onion, diced
- 1 teaspoon salt
- 1 cup tomato paste
- 1/2 cup water

Combine the venison, bacon, bread crumbs, bell pepper, white pepper, mustard, Worcestershire sauce, garlic powder, curry powder, chowchow, canned tomatoes, eggs, onion and salt in a large bowl and mix well. Shape the meat mixture into a loaf in a greased baking dish.

Bake meat loaf at 300 degrees for 2 hours. Combine tomato paste and water in a medium bowl and mix well. Baste meat loaf with this mixture occasionally during baking. Makes 6 servings.

Creole Eggplant and Venison Bake

- 2 eggplant, peeled and chopped
- 1 pound ground venison
- 2 onions, diced
- 2 tablespoons olive oil
- 1 egg, beaten
- Dash Creole seasoning
- 1 cup Italian seasoned bread crumbs

Bring the eggplant and water to cover to a boil in a large saucepan. Boil for 5 minutes. Drain.

Brown the ground venison and onions in olive oil in a large skillet. Add the eggplant, egg and Creole seasoning and mix well. Place mixture in a greased baking dish. Top with bread crumbs. Bake at 350 degrees for 15 minutes or until very hot. Makes 4 to 6 servings.

Venison and Bean Casserole

1½ pounds ground venison
½ pound ground beef
1 garlic clove, thinly sliced
1½ cups minced onions
2 green bell peppers, chopped
1 beef bouillon cube
1 teaspoon chili powder
2 cups canned tomatoes
2 cups cooked kidney beans
1 cup rice, rinsed

Brown the venison and ground beef in a large skillet. Add the garlic, onions, bell peppers, bouillon cube and chili powder and mix well. Cook for 5 minutes. Remove from heat and add undrained tomatoes and beans and mix well. Add the rice and mix well. Pour mixture into a 2-quart or larger baking dish. Bake, covered, at 375 degrees for 1 hour or until rice is tender. Makes 6 to 8 servings.

Spaghetti for a Crowd

8 pounds ground venison
1 pound green bell peppers, diced
1½ pounds onions, diced
1½ ribs celery, chopped
1 pound shredded Cheddar cheese
½ gallon tomato paste
½ cup flour
4 teaspoons oregano
2 tablespoons salt
3 tablespoons brown sugar
2 tablespoons dry mustard
2 tablespoons white pepper
1 tablespoon curry powder
1 tablespoon garlic powder
2 tablespoons chili powder
2 pounds spaghetti
Salt to taste

Brown the venison in a large stockpot or Dutch oven, stirring until crumbly. Add the bell peppers, onions and celery and cook until tender. Add the cheese and cook until cheese is melted, stirring constantly. Add the tomato paste, flour, oregano, salt, brown sugar, dry mustard, pepper, curry powder, garlic powder and chili powder. Cook over low heat for 1 hour.

Prepare the spaghetti in boiling salted water according to package directions. Serve the sauce over the spaghetti. Makes 40 servings.

Venison Burgers

2 pounds ground venison
1/2 cup minced onion
1 garlic clove, minced
1/4 cup chopped parsley
1/2 cup dry red wine
2 tablespoons soy sauce
Salt and pepper to taste

Combine the venison, onion, garlic, parsley, wine, soy sauce, salt and pepper in a bowl and mix well. Form into 6 patties. Grill or broil until cooked through. Cook quickly, as meat will toughen if overcooked. Serve with burger buns and condiments. Makes 6 servings.

Venison Party Meatballs

4 pounds ground venison
1 pound bulk sausage
4 slices dry bread, soaked in milk
2 eggs, beaten
1 medium white onion, grated or puréed
Garlic salt, salt, pepper and parsley flakes to taste
Vegetable oil for frying
1 medium onion, grated
1/4 cup vegetable oil
1/4 cup vinegar
1/4 cup packed brown sugar
1/2 cup lemon juice
2 cups ketchup
2 cups water
1 tablespoon prepared mustard

Combine the venison, sausage, bread, eggs, 1 onion, garlic salt, salt, pepper and parsley flakes in a large bowl and mix well. Roll the meat mixture into small balls. Fry meatballs in hot oil in a skillet. Drain and place in baking dishes.

Combine 1 onion, 1/4 cup oil, vinegar, brown sugar, lemon juice, ketchup, water, mustard and salt in a separate skillet. Simmer for 25 minutes. Pour over meatballs. Bake at 350 degrees for 30 minutes. Makes 225 meatballs or about 40 servings.

Note: These meatballs freeze well after cooking.

German-Style Venison and Pork Meatballs

1 pound ground venison
1/2 pound ground pork
1 egg, beaten
1/2 cup fine dry bread crumbs
1/2 cup mashed potatoes
1 teaspoon Lawry's seasoned salt
1/2 teaspoon pepper
1/2 teaspoon brown sugar
1/4 teaspoon allspice
1/8 teaspoon ground ginger
1/4 teaspoon ground nutmeg
1/8 teaspoon ground cloves
1/4 cup (1/2 stick) butter

Combine the venison, pork, egg, bread crumbs, potatoes, seasoned salt, pepper, brown sugar, allspice, ginger, nutmeg and cloves in a large bowl and mix well. Shape mixture into 1-inch balls. Brown in butter in a large skillet over medium heat. Cover and simmer over low heat for 15 minutes. Serve with white or wild rice or mashed potatoes. Makes 6 servings.

Cross Venison Jerky

4 pounds venison
2 quarts water
2 tablespoons liquid smoke flavoring
1/3 cup pickling salt
1 tablespoon garlic powder
4 beef bouillon cubes
1 tablespoon pepper
1 teaspoon Lawry's seasoned salt
1 tablespoon Tabasco sauce
1 tablespoon Worcestershire sauce

Cut the venison into thin strips. Combine the water, liquid smoke flavoring, pickling salt, garlic powder, bouillon cubes, pepper, seasoned salt, Tabasco sauce and Worcestershire sauce in a large container. Add venison and mix well. Refrigerate for 1 1/2 hours. Remove the meat from marinade, discard the marinade and rinse in cold water. Place the meat in a dehydrator set at 140 degrees for 6 hours. Or you may place meat on a baking sheet in an oven set at low temperature (below 200 degrees) for 4 to 6 hours. Leave the oven door slightly ajar.
Makes about 8 servings.

Cross Venison Soup

3 pounds venison, cut into small stewing pieces
3 quarts cold water
2 carrots
1 rib celery
1 tablespoon salt
1 tablespoon pepper
1 tablespoon chopped parsley
4 green onions
2 large potatoes, diced
Dash Tabasco sauce

Combine the venison and cold water in a stockpot. Bring to a boil over medium-high heat. Add the carrots, celery, salt, pepper, parsley, green onions and potatoes. Simmer, covered, until meat is tender. Season with the Tabasco sauce. Makes 8 to 10 servings.

Cross Smoked Turkey

1 wild turkey
1/2 cup peanut oil
1 teaspoon white pepper
1 cup sparkling lemon-lime soda
1 cup honey

Brush the turkey with peanut oil and sprinkle with pepper. Place a piece of wide heavy-duty aluminum foil in a large roasting pan. Place turkey breast side up on foil. Pour the lemon-lime soda into cavity of turkey. Seal foil tightly. Bake at 300 degrees for 8 minutes per pound. Remove from the oven. Melt the honey over low heat in a saucepan. Baste the turkey with honey. Place on greased aluminum foil on the grill. Smoke at medium over hickory chips until turkey is golden brown. Makes 8 to 12 servings.

Roasted Wild Turkey

1 (10- to 12-pound) wild turkey
2 tablespoons salt
1/2 teaspoon pepper
1 tablespoon vinegar
1 cup diced celery
1/2 cup diced onion
1/2 potato, diced
2 garlic cloves, minced
1/2 cup diced green bell pepper
1/2 cup (1 stick) butter, melted
1/2 cup flour

Rinse and dry the turkey. Combine the salt, pepper and vinegar and brush turkey inside and out with mixture. Combine the celery, onion, potato, garlic and bell pepper in a bowl. Stuff this mixture into cavity of turkey. Place the turkey on a rack in a roasting pan. Combine the melted butter and flour in a bowl and mix well. Baste turkey with this mixture occasionally during cooking. Roast at 325 degrees for 3 hours or until meat is tender. To test a turkey for doneness, rotate one leg; if it turns easily at the joint, the meat should be tender. Makes 12 to 18 servings.

Fruit-Stuffed Wild Turkey

1 cup chopped tart apple
2 tablespoons minced onion
1 cup chopped celery
1/4 cup pecans, chopped
1/2 cup raisins
3/4 cup bacon drippings
3 cups dry bread crumbs
Salt and pepper to taste
1/8 teaspoon thyme
1/2 cup water
1 wild turkey
Butter

Cook the apple, onion, celery, pecans and raisins in hot bacon drippings in a large skillet until tender. Add the bread crumbs, salt, pepper, thyme and water and mix well. Pack the stuffing into turkey cavity. Rub turkey skin all over with butter, then season with salt and pepper. Roast at 325 degrees for 20 minutes per pound. You may baste occasionally with a mixture of equal parts butter and white wine. Makes 8 to 12 servings.

Delta Baked Turkey

1 large or 2 small wild turkeys
1/3 cup honey
1 teaspoon salt
1 teaspoon pepper
6 tablespoons butter, melted
3/4 cup chopped onion
1 1/2 cups chicken broth
1 1/2 cups white wine
1 teaspoon parsley flakes

Cut the turkey into serving pieces and brush with honey. Sprinkle with salt and pepper. Arrange in a large baking pan (or 2 pans if needed). Bake at 425 degrees for 40 minutes, basting often with butter. Combine the onion, broth, wine and parsley in a bowl. Pour over turkey. Reduce heat to 225 degrees. Bake, covered, for 1 1/2 hours or until turkey is cooked through. Makes 12 to 15 servings.

Sweet-and-Sour Wild Turkey

- 1 wild turkey, cut into serving pieces
- 1 quart water
- 1 large onion, chopped
- 2 garlic cloves, minced
- 1 bay leaf
- 2 whole cloves
- 1 teaspoon prepared mustard
- 2 teaspoons salt
- 10 peppercorns
- 2 tablespoons cornstarch
- 1/4 cup sugar
- 1/3 cup vinegar

Place the turkey in a large roasting pan with the water. Add the onion, garlic, bay leaf, cloves, mustard, salt and peppercorns. Bake, covered, at 250 degrees for 2 hours. Remove the turkey. Strain the broth. Combine the broth and cornstarch in a large heatproof pan (or in the roasting pan). Add the sugar and vinegar. Cook over medium-low heat until sauce thickens, stirring constantly. Add the turkey to pan and simmer for 20 minutes. Remove the bay leaf before serving. Makes 8 servings.

Turkey Breast and Cream Gravy

1 wild turkey breast
3 cups milk
1 cup flour
1/2 teaspoon salt
1/2 teaspoon pepper
1 cup vegetable oil
1 teaspoon minced onion

Cut the turkey into cubes. Combine the turkey and milk in a large bowl and marinate, covered, in the refrigerator for 2 to 4 hours. Remove the turkey from the milk and reserve the milk. Coat the turkey in a mixture of flour, salt and pepper. Brown the meat in oil in a large skillet over medium heat. Drain excess oil from the skillet. Add the reserved milk and onion to the skillet. Cook until the gravy is thickened, stirring constantly and adding more flour if needed for the desired consistency. Serve the turkey and gravy over hot cooked rice. Makes 4 servings.

Fried Wild Turkey Breast

1 wild turkey breast
2 cups milk
3 cups baking mix
12 ounces beer
2 tablespoons sugar
3 cups peanut oil

Skin the turkey and remove the bones. Cut meat into 1-inch cubes. Combine with the milk in a large bowl and let stand for 30 to 45 minutes. Combine the baking mix, beer and sugar in a large bowl and mix to form a thin batter. Heat oil in a skillet to 375 degrees. Remove the meat from the milk. Dip into the batter. Fry in hot oil until golden brown. Drain on paper towels. Serve with wooden picks. Makes 6 servings.

Turkey Burger

1 turkey, deboned
1$^1/_4$ cups cubed salt pork
1 teaspoon salt
$^1/_3$ teaspoon pepper
1 teaspoon sausage seasoning
$^1/_2$ teaspoon onion salt
Dash garlic salt
Flour

Combine the turkey, pork, salt, pepper, sausage seasoning, onion salt, garlic salt and flour in a large bowl and mix well. Put through a meat grinder or a food processor to grind. Shape the mixture into patties. Coat the patties with flour and fry until golden brown. Makes about 30 burgers.

Hot Turkey Casserole

2 cups diced cooked turkey
1 rib celery, chopped
1 (10-ounce) can cream of chicken soup
$^1/_2$ teaspoon salt
1 large onion, chopped
2 tablespoons lemon juice
$^1/_4$ teaspoon pepper
$^3/_4$ cup mayonnaise
5 hard-cooked eggs, chopped
$^1/_3$ cup sweet pickles, chopped
1 cup crushed potato chips

Combine the turkey, celery, soup, salt, onion, lemon juice, pepper, mayonnaise, eggs and pickles in a large bowl and mix well. Spoon into a greased baking dish. Sprinkle the potato chips over the top. Bake at 325 degrees for 20 to 25 minutes. Makes 4 to 6 servings.

Small Game

Small Game
Small Game
Small Game
Small Game
Small Game
Small Game
Small Game
Small Game

Baked Squirrel

4 squirrels, cut into serving pieces
2 cups flour
Salt, seasoned salt and pepper to taste
2 cups peanut oil
1 (10-ounce) can beef bouillon
1/4 teaspoon Worcestershire sauce
2 tablespoons parsley, chopped
2 tablespoons onion juice
1 garlic clove, minced
1 small bay leaf

Coat the squirrel in flour combined with salt, seasoned salt and pepper. Brown in hot oil in a large ovenproof skillet or roasting pan. Drain. Add the bouillon, Worcestershire sauce, parsley, onion juice, garlic and bay leaf to skillet. Simmer, covered, over medium heat for 45 minutes. Reduce the temperature to low and continue cooking for 45 minutes or until tender. Discard the bay leaf before serving. Makes 4 to 6 servings.

Crumb-Coated Squirrel

2 squirrels, cut into serving pieces
1 1/2 quarts water
1 bay leaf
3 tablespoons prepared mustard
3/4 cup (1 1/2 sticks) margarine, melted
3/4 cup mayonnaise
1 (8-ounce) package seasoned bread crumbs
1/2 teaspoon salt
1/4 teaspoon black pepper
Dash red pepper

Boil the squirrel in the water in a stockpot with a bay leaf until tender. Drain; discard the bay leaf. Combine the mustard, margarine and mayonnaise in a shallow dish. Dip the squirrel into margarine mixture, then coat with bread crumbs mixed with the salt, black pepper and red pepper. Place in a greased baking dish. Bake at 350 degrees for 30 minutes. Makes 4 servings.

Fried Squirrel

4 squirrels, cut into serving pieces
3 cups milk
$1^1/2$ cups flour
Lawry's seasoned salt to taste
4 eggs, beaten
3 cups peanut oil

Combine the squirrel and milk in a large bowl and refrigerate for 4 to 6 hours. Remove the squirrel from the milk, reserving milk. Combine the flour with seasoned salt in a bowl. Coat the squirrel with this mixture. Then dip into the eggs and roll in flour again. Brown in 375-degree peanut oil in a large skillet, covered. Remove the lid toward the end of cooking so squirrel can brown. Drain all but 1 tablespoon of cooking oil from skillet.

Place the squirrel in a pressure cooker with 1 inch of water. Cook squirrel at 15 pounds pressure for 15 to 18 minutes, using manufacturer's directions. Remove the squirrel from pressure cooker, reserving cooking liquid.

Add the reserved cooking liquid to skillet. Add the reserved milk. Simmer over low heat until thickened. Serve squirrel and gravy on biscuits or toast.
Makes 4 to 6 servings.

Deep-Fried Squirrel

3 squirrels, cut into serving pieces
3 cups milk
$1^1/2$ cups water
3 eggs
6 tablespoons flour
1 teaspoon Lawry's seasoned salt
3 cups peanut oil

Combine the squirrel and 2 cups of the milk in a large bowl and let stand for 1 hour; drain. Combine the squirrel with the water in a pressure cooker. Seal and cook at 15 pounds pressure for 15 minutes, according to manufacturer's directions. Remove squirrel from cooker. Combine the eggs and remaining 1 cup milk in a bowl. Combine the flour and seasoned salt in a bowl or on waxed paper. Dip squirrel into egg mixture, then coat with flour mixture. Deep-fry in 375-degree oil in a large skillet until cooked through. Makes 5 or 6 servings.

Country-Style Squirrel

2 cups flour
Salt and pepper to taste
2 squirrels, cut into serving pieces
6 tablespoons vegetable oil
2 cups water

Combine the flour, salt and pepper in a paper or plastic bag. Add the squirrel and shake to coat. Fry in hot oil in a skillet until golden brown. Remove from skillet. Drain all but 2 tablespoons oil. Add the water to the skillet and bring to a boil. Return the squirrel to skillet. Reduce heat to low. Cook, covered, for about 1 hour or until meat is falling from bones. Makes 2 to 4 servings.

Squirrel and Quick Dumplings

4 squirrels, cut into serving pieces
12 cups water
1/4 cup (1/2 stick) margarine
1/2 teaspoon salt
1/2 teaspoon pepper
1 (10-count) can refrigerated biscuits
1 cup flour

Combine the squirrel, water, margarine, salt and pepper in a pot. Boil until squirrel is tender, adding more water if needed. Remove the squirrel from the broth, reserving broth. Debone the meat and return to pot. Bring liquid to a simmer.

Separate the biscuits. Place each on a floured surface and roll thin with a rolling pin. Cut into 1-inch squares. Drop into boiling stock. Cook over medium heat until dumplings are cooked through. Makes 4 to 6 servings.

Squirrels and Homemade Dumplings

3 squirrels, cut into serving pieces
1/4 cup (1/2 stick) margarine
2 cups flour
1/4 teaspoon baking soda
3/4 teaspoon salt

Boil the squirrel in water to cover in a stockpot until tender. (Or cook in 1 inch of water in a pressure cooker at 15 pounds pressure for 18 to 20 minutes or until tender.) Debone the meat and return to stock. Add the margarine to stock and bring to a boil. Combine the flour, baking soda and salt in a bowl. Add 1 cup boiling stock to bowl. Stir until a soft dough forms. Roll the dough very thin on a floured surface with a rolling pin. Cut into small pieces and drop into boiling stock. Simmer, covered, for 25 minutes. Makes 4 or 5 servings.

Squirrel Mulligan

6 large squirrels, cut into serving pieces
2 cups (4 sticks) butter or margarine
1/4 teaspoon red pepper
3 teaspoons salt
6 medium potatoes, chopped
1 cup chopped celery
6 medium onions, chopped
1 quart tomatoes
1 (15-ounce) can cream-style corn
3 tablespoons sugar
1 cup bread crumbs

Combine the squirrel and water to cover in a large pot. Add the butter, red pepper and salt. Cook over low heat until the meat is tender. Debone the meat and return to the broth. Add the potatoes, celery and onions. Cook until the potatoes are tender. Add the tomatoes, corn and sugar. Bring to a boil. Simmer over low heat until the vegetables are falling apart. Add the bread crumbs and cook until thickened. Makes 8 to 12 servings.

Squirrel Fricassee

2 dressed squirrels, cut into serving pieces
1 1/2 cups flour
1/2 cup bacon drippings
3 cups chicken broth
1 teaspoon salt
1/2 teaspoon pepper
3/4 cup chopped onion

Coat the squirrel with flour. Brown in bacon drippings in a Dutch oven. Add the broth, salt, pepper and onion to the pan. Simmer for 1 1/2 hours or until squirrel is tender. Serve with biscuits or dumplings. Makes 3 or 4 servings

Cross Brunswick Stew

5 dressed squirrels, cut into serving pieces
1 bay leaf
Dash red pepper
1/2 teaspoon salt
Dash black pepper
1 (2 1/2-pound) hen
4 large onions, diced
2 1/2 cups sliced okra (optional)
1 lemon, diced
3 pounds potatoes, peeled and diced
1 (15-ounce) can corn
2 (14-ounce) cans whole tomatoes, chopped
1 pound cooked ham, diced
1 tablespoon black pepper
1 tablespoon garlic powder
1 teaspoon MSG
1 (8-ounce) bottle ketchup
2 tablespoons salt
1/3 cup Worcestershire sauce

Boil the squirrel in water to cover in a stockpot with bay leaf, red pepper, 1/2 teaspoon salt and dash of black pepper. Cook until tender. Remove meat from the liquid and debone, reserving liquid. Set aside. Cook the hen in the liquid until tender. Remove and debone. Set aside. Add the onions, okra, lemon, potatoes and corn and simmer until the potatoes are tender. Add the tomatoes, ham, 1 tablespoon black pepper, garlic powder, MSG, ketchup, 2 tablespoons salt and Worcestershire sauce. Return the squirrel and chicken to pot. Simmer over low heat for 5 hours. Discard the bay leaf. May be frozen for later use. Makes about 15 servings.

Squirrel Stew

2 tablespoons butter
1 large onion, thinly sliced
1 (16-ounce) can stewed tomatoes
Salt and freshly ground pepper to taste
2 squirrels, cut into serving pieces
Flour for thickening

Melt the butter in a large saucepan over medium heat. Add the onion. Cook until the onion is tender, stirring occasionally. Add the undrained tomatoes, salt and pepper and simmer for 5 minutes. Add the squirrel and boiling water to cover. Cook over low heat until the squirrel is tender.

Estimate the amount of liquid in the pan and measure 1 tablespoon of flour for each cup of liquid. Mix a small amount of cooking liquid with the flour in a cup or bowl to make a thin paste. Pour the paste into the saucepan. Cook for 5 minutes or until liquid is thickened, stirring constantly. Makes 4 servings.

Squirrel with Rice and Potatoes

2 old squirrels, cut into serving pieces
1 cup vegetable oil
1 onion, chopped
1 green bell pepper, chopped
1/4 cup chopped celery
1 garlic clove, chopped
1 cup rice
3 medium potatoes, chopped
Salt and pepper to taste
1 quart (about) water

Brown the squirrel in the oil in a large skillet. Remove the squirrel from skillet to a pressure cooker, reserving the pan drippings. Cook for 15 minutes according to manufacturer's directions. Sauté the onion, bell pepper, celery and garlic in the reserved pan drippings. Add the meat, rice, potatoes, salt and pepper to the skillet. Add about 1 quart water. Cook, covered, over low heat for about 2 hours or until squirrel is tender.
Makes 4 to 6 servings.

Squirrel and Rice Bake

2 squirrels, cut into serving pieces
Salt and pepper to taste
1/2 cup (1 stick) margarine
1 cup rice
2 cups broth (chicken, beef, squirrel)
1 envelope onion soup mix

Parboil the squirrel in water to cover in a large stockpot with salt, pepper and margarine until tender. (Or cook in a pressure cooker using manufacturer's directions.) Debone the meat. Combine with the rice, broth and soup mix in a bowl. Pour into a baking dish. Bake at 325 degrees for 30 minutes. Makes 4 servings.

Rabbit Piquant

4 1/2 to 5 pounds rabbit, cut into serving pieces
Flour
Salt, black pepper and red pepper to taste
1 cup vegetable oil
2 cups chopped onions
2 cups chopped celery
1 green bell pepper, chopped
1 (16-ounce) can tomato juice
1 (16-ounce) can whole tomatoes
5 cups water
1 (8-ounce) can mushrooms
1 teaspoon sugar
6 garlic cloves, minced
1/4 cup chopped green onion tops
1/4 cup chopped parsley

Sprinkle the rabbit with flour, salt, black pepper and red pepper. Fry, covered, in hot oil in a large heavy pan over medium-low heat for 30 minutes or until the rabbit is tender, turning occasionally. Remove from the pan. Cook onions, celery and bell pepper in pan drippings until tender. Add the tomato juice, undrained tomatoes and water and mix well. Cook over medium heat until the oil floats above the tomatoes. Return the rabbit to the pan and add the mushrooms, sugar and garlic. Season to taste. Cook for 25 minutes. Add the green onions and parsley. Serve over hot cooked rice. You may substitute an equal amount of duck for the rabbit in this recipe. Makes 4 servings.

Rabbit Paprikash

3 pounds rabbit, cut into serving pieces
Flour
Salt and pepper to taste
1 cup vegetable oil
1/4 cup chopped onion
1 tablespoon paprika
1/2 cup hot water
2 cups sour cream
1 (12-ounce) package wide egg noodles, cooked
2 tablespoons poppy seeds
1 tablespoon butter

Coat the rabbit with flour combined with salt and pepper. Fry in hot oil in a large skillet until well browned. Add the onion, paprika and hot water to skillet and mix well. Simmer over low heat for about 1 to 1 1/2 hours or until the rabbit is tender. Remove the rabbit from skillet. Add the sour cream to the liquid in the skillet. Heat to a boil, stirring constantly. Add salt and pepper to taste. If the mixture seems thin, add flour 1 teaspoon at a time and cook until the mixture thickens, stirring constantly. Return the rabbit to the skillet.

Combine the hot cooked noodles with the poppy seeds and butter in a bowl and mix well. Place the noodles on a large serving platter. Top with the meat and sauce. Serve with sweet-sour red cabbage. Makes 8 servings.

Fried Wild Rabbit

2 rabbits, cut into serving pieces
Juice of 1 lemon
Salt and pepper to taste
1/4 teaspoon oregano
2 eggs
2 tablespoons milk
1/2 cup flour
1/2 cup bread crumbs
Peanut oil for frying

Combine the rabbit, lemon juice and water to cover in a pan and boil for 10 minutes. Drain, pat dry and sprinkle the rabbit with salt, pepper and oregano. Beat the eggs and milk in a bowl. Coat the meat with flour, then dip into the egg mixture, then roll in the bread crumbs. Heat 1/2 inch oil in a large heavy skillet. Brown the rabbit on all sides. Reduce the heat. Cover and cook for about 20 minutes or until rabbit is tender. Makes 6 servings.

Browned Rabbit

4 pounds rabbit, cut into serving pieces
Salt and pepper to taste
1 cup flour
2 cups vegetable oil
3 tablespoons flour

Combine the rabbit and water to cover in a large pot and bring to a boil. Boil until the rabbit is tender. Remove the rabbit and reserve the cooking liquid.

Combine the salt, pepper and 1 cup flour in a bowl. Coat meat with flour mixture. Cook in hot oil in a large skillet over medium heat for about 20 to 30 minutes or until well browned. Remove rabbit from skillet and keep warm. Pour off all but 3 tablespoons drippings from skillet. Add 3 tablespoons flour to drippings. Cook until mixture bubbles, stirring constantly. Add 3 cups broth gradually. Cook over low heat until thickened, stirring occasionally. Serve with rabbit. Makes 4 servings.

Simmered Rabbit and Gravy

2 rabbits, cut into serving pieces
1/3 teaspoon garlic powder
1 bay leaf
Dash red pepper
1/2 teaspoon black pepper
1 teaspoon salt
1 cup flour
Salt and black pepper to taste
2 tablespoons dry mustard
1/2 teaspoon curry powder
1 cup vegetable oil
1 1/2 cups milk

Combine the rabbit, water to cover, garlic powder, bay leaf, red pepper, 1/2 teaspoon black pepper and 1 teaspoon salt in a pot. Bring to a boil. Cook until tender. Remove meat from liquid and pat dry.

Combine the flour, salt and black pepper to taste, mustard and curry powder in a bowl. Coat the rabbit with flour mixture. Fry in hot oil in a skillet until golden brown. Drain the oil from the skillet. Add the milk to the skillet. Simmer, covered, for 30 minutes, stirring occasionally. Makes 8 to 12 servings.

Rabbit with Raisin Sauce

2 rabbits, cut into serving pieces
1/2 cup white vinegar
2 teaspoons salt
1 tablespoon dried minced onion
4 whole cloves
2 bay leaves
1/2 teaspoon ground allspice
1/2 cup raisins
1/4 cup packed brown sugar
2 tablespoons flour
1 cup water

Combine the rabbit and cool water to cover in a deep pot. Add 1/4 cup of the vinegar. Bring to a boil. Boil for 5 minutes. Drain and discard water. Cover rabbit with cool water. Add remaining 1/4 cup vinegar, salt, onion, cloves, bay leaves and allspice. Bring to a boil. Lower heat and simmer until rabbit is nearly tender. Add the raisins and brown sugar and mix well. Continue cooking until rabbit is tender. Remove the rabbit from pot. Combine the flour with a little water in a cup and mix until smooth. Add the remaining water, stirring until a thin paste forms. Pour into the pot and cook until the liquid is thickened, stirring constantly. Add the rabbit to the pot and heat through. Makes 6 to 8 servings.

Barbecued Rabbit

2 onions, minced
1 garlic clove, minced
3 green bell peppers, minced
1 cup water
1 cup white vinegar
1/2 cup ketchup
1/2 cup Worcestershire sauce
1/4 cup (1/2 stick) butter
1 teaspoon salt
1/2 teaspoon cayenne pepper
2 dressed wild rabbits, cut into serving pieces

Combine the onions, garlic, bell peppers, water, vinegar, ketchup, Worcestershire sauce, butter, salt and cayenne pepper in a saucepan and mix well. Cook over medium-high heat for 5 minutes. Arrange the rabbit in a baking pan in a single layer. Pour the sauce over the rabbit. Bake at 300 degrees for 3 hours or until the rabbit is tender, turning occasionally. Makes 6 servings.

Spanish-Style Rabbit in Wine

2 rabbits, cut into serving pieces
1 white onion, chopped
2 carrots, diced
1 bay leaf
1 (750-milliliter) bottle red wine
6 tablespoons butter
Salt and pepper to taste
1 white onion, chopped
1/2 cup chopped ham
1 (7-ounce) can mushrooms
1 tablespoon butter

Arrange the rabbit, 1 onion, carrots and bay leaf in a deep dish. Cover with red wine. Refrigerate for 24 hours.

Remove the rabbit from the wine, reserving the wine marinade but discarding the bay leaf. Sauté in 6 tablespoons hot butter in a large skillet until browned all over. Season with salt and pepper. Strain the wine marinade into the skillet with the meat. Bring to a boil, reduce heat, and simmer, covered, until meat is tender.

Sauté 1 onion, ham and mushrooms in 1 tablespoon butter in a skillet. To serve, place meat in a serving dish. Top with sautéed onion mixture. Pour red wine pan juices over meat. Makes 6 servings.

Stewed Wild Rabbit with Dumplings

1 large rabbit, cut into serving pieces
Salt and pepper to taste
1 cup flour
1 1/4 cups vegetable oil
2 quarts water
6 medium onions, quartered
6 large carrots, diced
4 teaspoons salt
2 cups flour
1 tablespoon baking powder
1/2 teaspoon salt
1 tablespoon melted butter
1 cup milk

Sprinkle the rabbit with salt and pepper to taste, then coat with 1 cup flour. Brown in hot oil in a Dutch oven. Drain the pan drippings. Add the water and simmer, covered, for about 1 1/2 hours. Add the onions, carrots and 4 teaspoons salt to the pot. Simmer for 1 hour.

Sift 2 cups flour with the baking powder and 1/2 teaspoon salt into a large bowl. Add the butter and milk and stir quickly to mix. Drop teaspoonfuls of mixture into hot cooking liquid with rabbit. Cook, covered, for 10 minutes. Makes 12 servings.

Rabbit Pie

- 1/4 cup (1/2 stick) butter or margarine
- 1/4 cup chopped onion
- 1/2 cup chopped green bell pepper
- 1/4 cup sifted flour
- 2 cups rabbit broth, or 2 cups water plus 4 chicken bouillon cubes
- Salt and pepper to taste
- 3 cups chopped cooked rabbit
- 1 cup flour, sifted
- 1/2 teaspoon salt
- 1/2 cup shortening
- 2 to 3 tablespoons ice water

Heat the butter in a large skillet. Add the onion and bell pepper and cook for about 5 minutes or until tender, stirring frequently. Add 1/4 cup flour and mix well. Add the broth and cook until thick, stirring frequently. Add the salt, pepper and rabbit and mix well. Pour mixture into a shallow baking dish.

Combine 1 cup flour and 1/2 teaspoon salt in a bowl. Cut in shortening with a pastry cutter or two knives until mixture resembles coarse crumbs. Add 2 tablespoons ice water and stir until mixture holds together, adding more water if needed.

Roll the pastry on a floured surface into a shape that will just overlap the edges of the baking container. Fit the crust over the dish, crimping the edges. Prick holes or cut slits in the top for steam to escape. Bake at 425 degrees for 15 to 20 minutes or until the crust is brown and the sauce bubbles. Makes 4 to 6 servings.

Rabbit Chili

- 1 dressed rabbit, cut into serving pieces
- 1 garlic clove, minced
- 2 tablespoons olive oil
- 1 teaspoon chili powder
- 1 cup hot water
- 1/2 teaspoon salt
- 1/2 teaspoon pepper
- 1 (6-ounce) can tomato paste
- 1 (16-ounce) can kidney beans
- 1 teaspoon ground cumin
- 1 tablespoon shredded Cheddar cheese

Brown the rabbit and garlic in olive oil in a large skillet. Add the chili powder and mix well. Add the hot water, salt, pepper, tomato paste, kidney beans and cumin and mix well. Simmer, covered, over very low heat for 2 hours. Spoon the mixture into a baking dish and sprinkle with cheese. Bake at 350 degrees for 15 minutes.
Makes 6 servings.

Rabbit Salad

3 cups chopped cooked rabbit
4 whole sweet pickles, chopped
3 tablespoons pickle juice
1/2 cup finely chopped celery
1/2 cup mayonnaise
4 hard-cooked eggs, chopped
1 onion, finely chopped
Dash salt

Combine the rabbit, pickles, pickle juice, celery, mayonnaise, eggs, onion and salt in a large bowl and mix well. You may need to use additional mayonnaise to bind or pickle juice to thin the mixture and give it flavor. Makes 4 cups.

Grilled Beaver Tail

1 beaver tail, cleaned
Salt and pepper to taste
Melted butter

Grill the whole beaver tail until skin blisters. Remove from heat and let cool. Remove and discard the skin. Return to the grill and cook until tender. Season with salt, pepper and melted butter. Makes 1 serving.

Preparing Beaver

Before cooking a beaver, it's important to remove scent kernels. There is one behind the knee of each back leg, one on each side between the shoulder blades and the rib cage and there are two in the neck. The neck kernels are hard to find. Rather than hunting for them, the best way to make sure they are removed is to cut the neck off close to the body. Be sure to remove all surface fat from the carcass before cooking.

Roast Beaver

- 1 beaver, cut into serving pieces
- 2 cups salt
- Baking soda
- Salt and pepper to taste
- 6 large sweet potatoes, cut into chunks
- 2 large onions, cut into chunks
- 1 bunch celery, cut into chunks
- 1 to 2 pounds bacon slices

Combine the beaver, water to cover and 2 cups salt in a large container. Refrigerate for at least 4 hours and up to 8 hours. Drain. Rinse the beaver in cold water. Combine the beaver and water to cover in a large pot. Add 1 teaspoon baking soda per gallon of water. Bring to a boil. Boil for 10 minutes. Remove the beaver from the water. Sprinkle with salt and pepper to taste. Place the beaver in a roasting pan with sweet potatoes, onions and celery. Cover the meat with bacon. Bake, covered, at 350 degrees until tender. Makes 25 servings.

Oven-Barbecued Beaver

- 1 beaver, cleaned
- 2 cups salt
- 2 cups apple juice
- 1 tablespoon red pepper
- 1 1/2 quarts hickory smoke-flavored barbecue sauce
- 1/2 teaspoon prepared mustard
- 2 bunches green onions with tops
- Red pepper to taste
- 1 to 2 pounds sliced bacon
- 1/2 cup (1 stick) melted butter

Remove all visible fat from the beaver. Cut the beaver into small pieces. Combine the beaver, water to cover and salt in a large container and soak for 8 hours. Drain. Wash the meat in cool water. Place in a pressure cooker. Add the apple juice and 1 tablespoon red pepper. Cook at 15 pounds pressure according to manufacturer's directions for 30 minutes. Remove the beaver from pressure cooker and debone. Combine the meat, barbecue sauce, mustard, green onions and red pepper to taste in a large bowl and mix well. Refrigerate for 3 hours. Spoon the mixture into a baking dish. Cover the meat with bacon slices and bake at 325 degrees for 30 minutes, basting with butter if meat appears dry. Makes about 25 servings.

Cross Barbecued Beaver

1 beaver
2 cups salt
1 tablespoon black pepper
1 teaspoon red pepper
2 bay leaves
2 (18-ounce) bottles barbecue sauce
2 white onions
2 green bell peppers
8 slices bacon

Combine the beaver, water to cover and salt in a large container. Refrigerate for 8 hours.

Drain the beaver and discard the liquid. Rinse the beaver in cold water. Place in a large pot with water to cover. Add the black pepper, red pepper and bay leaves. Bring to a boil. Boil until the meat is tender. Remove the beaver from the liquid and debone.

Combine meat with barbecue sauce in a large plastic or glass container. Refrigerate for 8 hours.

Chop the onions and bell peppers. Add to the meat and mix well. Spoon into a baking dish. Top with the bacon. Bake at 350 degrees for 35 minutes.
Makes 25 servings.

Barbecued Beaver

2 beavers, cut into serving pieces
Garlic salt and red pepper to taste
3 onions, cut into chunks
1/2 bottle Tabasco sauce
2 (12-ounce) cans beer
Salt to taste
Barbecue sauce

Boil the beaver in water to cover in a large pot with garlic salt, red pepper, onions, Tabasco sauce and beer for about 2 hours or until tender. Add the salt near the end of the cooking time. Drain. Barbecue in the oven at 400 degrees or over hot coals with your favorite barbecue sauce.
Makes about 25 servings.

Roasted Raccoon

1 raccoon
2 tablespoons salt
1/2 teaspoon pepper
1 onion
3 carrots
3 bacon slices
1 cup broth

Clean the raccoon and remove all possible fat. Remove the scent nodules from under front legs and in the center of the back legs. Combine the raccoon, water to cover, salt, pepper, onion and carrots in a large pot. Bring to a boil and boil for 1 hour. Remove the meat from the cooking liquid, discarding the liquid and vegetables. Scrape off any remaining fat. Place the raccoon in a roasting pan. Arrange the bacon over meat. Add broth and roast, uncovered, at 375 degrees for 2 hours or until meat is tender.
Makes 8 to 10 servings.

Baked Raccoon and Vegetables

1 (6- to 8-pound) young raccoon
1 large onion, sliced
1 1/2 teaspoons salt
1/4 teaspoon pepper
1/4 teaspoon garlic salt
4 or 5 slices fresh pork or bacon
Dash Tabasco sauce
1 (16-ounce) can whole tomatoes
1/2 cup water
4 carrots, cut into chunks
4 sweet potatoes, cut into chunks
4 potatoes, cut into chunks

Remove all possible fat from the raccoon and remove the scent nodules located under front legs and in the center of the back legs. Combine the raccoon and water to cover in a large pot. Bring to a boil. Boil for 20 minutes. Remove from the liquid and let cool. Scrape off any remaining fat. Cut into serving pieces. Place the meat in a roasting pan with onion. Season with salt, pepper and garlic salt. Place pork or bacon over meat and season with Tabasco sauce. Add tomatoes and water to roasting pan. Bake, covered, at 325 degrees for 2 1/4 hours, adding more water as needed. Arrange carrots, sweet potatoes and potatoes around meat. Bake, covered, for about 45 minutes or until meat and vegetables are tender, adding more water as needed.
Makes 12 to 15 servings.

Baked Raccoon and Sweet Potatoes

1 raccoon
3 quarts water
2 small dried red peppers
2 bay leaves
1/2 teaspoon red pepper
1/2 teaspoon black pepper
1 teaspoon salt
6 sweet potatoes
2 tablespoons vegetable oil
1 tablespoon sugar
1 teaspoon cinnamon

Remove all possible fat from the raccoon and remove scent nodules located under front legs and in the center of the back legs. Combine the raccoon and water in a large pot. Add dried peppers, bay leaves, red pepper, black pepper and salt. Bring to a boil. Boil for 1 hour or until meat is tender. Drain, reserving some of the cooking liquid. Scrape any remaining fat from the raccoon.

Rub the sweet potatoes with the oil. Wrap individually in foil. Bake at 400 degrees for 45 minutes. Remove the foil. Let the sweet potatoes cool enough to handle. Peel and cut into halves. Sprinkle with the sugar and cinnamon.

Place the raccoon in a baking dish. Surround with sweet potato halves. Bake at 350 degrees for 40 minutes, basting often with the reserved cooking liquid.
Makes 12 servings.

Fricassee of Young Raccoon

2 young raccoons
Salt and pepper to taste
Vegetable oil
Flour
12 ounces water
1 large onion, sliced

Remove all possible fat from the raccoons and remove the scent nodules located under front legs and in the center of the back legs. Cut the raccoons into serving pieces. Sprinkle with salt and pepper and coat with the flour. Brown in hot oil in a heavy skillet. Combine a heaping tablespoon of flour with a small amount of the water, stirring to make a paste. Add the remaining water and mix well. Pour into skillet. Add enough additional water to cover the meat. Add the onion. Simmer, covered, for 1 hour. Makes 8 to 10 servings.

Raccoon in Sauce Piquant

1 raccoon
Salt and red pepper to taste
1 cup flour
Vegetable oil
2 cups water
1/3 cup flour
1/2 cup vegetable oil
4 large onions, chopped
1 garlic clove, chopped
1 green bell pepper, chopped
1/2 cup chopped celery
1/3 cup parsley, chopped
1 (10-ounce) can tomatoes with diced chiles
2 (16-ounce) cans whole tomatoes
2 cups water

Remove all fat and scent nodules from raccoon and cut into serving pieces. Sprinkle the raccoon with salt and red pepper and coat with the flour. Brown in hot oil in a large skillet. Place the raccoon in a pressure cooker with 2 cups water. Cook at 15 pounds pressure according to manufacturer's directions for 25 minutes. Remove and debone.

Combine 1/3 cup flour and 1/2 cup oil in a large skillet. Cook over medium-low heat until mixture browns slightly, stirring constantly. Add the onions, garlic, bell pepper, celery and parsley. Cook until the vegetables are tender. Add the tomatoes with chiles, undrained whole tomatoes and 2 cups water. Add the meat to the skillet and mix well. Simmer for 45 minutes, stirring occasionally. Serve over rice. Makes 15 servings.

German-Style Sweet-and-Sour Raccoon

1 dressed raccoon, cut into serving pieces
1 large onion, chopped
1 teaspoon dry mustard
1 teaspoon ground allspice
1 teaspoon salt
1/2 teaspoon pepper
3/4 cup ketchup
4 beef bouillon cubes
4 cups water
5 gingersnap cookies
3/4 cup vinegar
3/4 cup packed brown sugar

Bring the raccoon and water to cover to a boil in a pot. Boil for 1 hour or until meat is tender. Scrape off any remaining fat. Arrange the raccoon in a roasting pan. Add the onion to the pan. Sprinkle the mustard, allspice, salt and pepper over raccoon and onion. Heat the ketchup, bouillon cubes, water, gingersnap cookies, vinegar and brown sugar in a medium saucepan until cookies dissolve, stirring constantly. Pour over raccoon. Roast, covered, at 350 degrees for 3 hours or until meat is very tender. Makes 15 servings.

Simmered Nutria

1 cup self-rising flour
1 tablespoon Lawry's seasoned salt
Dash salt
Dash pepper
2 pounds nutria meat, cut into small serving pieces
1 cup peanut oil
1 cup water
1/2 cup finely chopped onion

Combine the flour, seasoned salt, salt and pepper in a bowl and mix well. Coat the nutria in the mixture, shaking off excess. Heat the oil in a Dutch oven over medium heat. Add the nutria and cook until brown, turning occasionally. Drain most of the oil. Add the water and onion to pot. Simmer, covered, until nutria is tender. Serve over hot cooked rice. Makes 4 servings.

Roast Opossum

1 dressed cleaned opossum
1 teaspoon salt
1 teaspoon pepper
1 onion, chopped
1/2 cup vegetable oil
1 opossum liver, chopped
1 cup bread crumbs
1/4 teaspoon Worcestershire sauce
1 hard-cooked egg, chopped
4 slices bacon
1 quart water

Trim all fat from opossum. Wipe with a damp cloth, remove any clinging hair and rinse inside and out. Rub the opossum with salt and pepper. Brown the opossum and onion in hot oil in a large skillet. Add the liver and cook until tender. Add the bread crumbs, Worcestershire sauce, egg and enough water to moisten. Stuff the mixture into the opossum. Tie with string to enclose stuffing. Arrange the opossum belly down in baking dish. Arrange the bacon over the meat. Add the water to baking dish. Roast, uncovered, at 350 degrees for about 2 1/2 hours or until very tender, basting every 15 minutes with pan juices. Makes 4 servings.

Opossum and Sweet Potatoes

1 (2 1/2-pound) opossum
2 1/2 teaspoons salt
Pepper to taste
Flour
1/2 cup water
4 medium sweet potatoes, peeled
2 tablespoons brown sugar

Trim all fat from the opossum. Wipe with a damp cloth, remove any clinging hair, then rinse inside and out.

Drain thoroughly. Rub the opossum with the salt mixed with pepper inside and out. Sprinkle with flour inside and out. Lay the opossum belly up in a roasting pan with a tight-fitting lid. Add the water, cover and bake at 350 degrees for 45 minutes to 1 hour.

Cut the sweet potatoes into halves lengthwise. Sprinkle lightly with brown sugar. Arrange around the opossum. Add more water if needed. Cook, covered, for 30 minutes longer. Makes 4 to 6 servings.

Baked Armadillo

2 pounds armadillo meat
Dash onion salt
Salt, pepper and lemon pepper to taste
Lemon juice
1/2 cup (1 stick) butter or margarine

Season the armadillo with onion salt, salt, pepper and lemon pepper. Sprinkle with the lemon juice and rub with some of the butter. Wrap in foil. Place in a baking pan. Bake at 325 degrees for 45 minutes. Remove the meat from the foil, add the remaining butter and cook until browned. For barbecued meat, baste with barbecue sauce over hot coals after removing the foil. Makes 4 to 6 servings.

Woodchuck in Tomato Sauce

1 dressed woodchuck
$1/2$ cup salt
4 mint leaves
$1/4$ cup vegetable oil
1 garlic clove, chopped
Salt and pepper to taste
$1/2$ cup vinegar
2 cups tomato sauce
Pinch of dried basil

Soak the woodchuck in a mixture of $1/2$ cup salt and enough cold water to cover in a large container for 8 hours. Drain. Cut into 8 serving pieces.

Bring meat and water to cover to a boil in a pot. Boil for 15 minutes. Drain, rinse and cover with more cold water. Soak for 8 hours longer. Drain, rinse and cover with water. Add mint leaves. Bring to a boil and boil for 45 minutes. Drain.

Brown meat in hot oil in a large skillet over medium-high heat. Add garlic, salt and pepper to taste and mix well. Add vinegar and mix well. Reduce heat and simmer, covered, for 8 minutes. Remove meat from skillet and put into a Dutch oven. Add tomato sauce and basil. Cook, covered, over moderate heat for $1\frac{1}{2}$ hours.
Makes 2 servings.

Fried Rattlesnake

2 pounds rattlesnake meat, cut into serving pieces
2 cups milk
3 eggs, beaten
1 cup flour
Salt and pepper to taste
Peanut oil

Marinate the rattlesnake meat in the milk in a large bowl for 1 hour. Remove and dip into beaten eggs in a separate bowl. Roll in flour mixed with salt and pepper to taste. Fry in 350-degree oil in a large skillet until golden brown. Drain on paper towels. Makes 4 to 6 servings.

Quail de Ridgepoint

1 (4-ounce) package (2 bags) crab boil
4 green onions
24 quail
1 (16-ounce) bottle Italian salad dressing
1 (10-ounce) bottle white wine Worcestershire sauce
1/4 cup soy sauce
1/4 cup red wine
Juice of 1 lemon
1 pound bacon slices
24 mushrooms
4 bell peppers, cored, cut into chunks
2 onions, cut into quarters and separated into chunks
24 cherry tomatoes
Creole seasoning

Bring a large pot of water to a boil with the crab boil and green onions. Turn off the heat and add the quail to the pot. Let stand for 15 to 20 minutes.

Combine the salad dressing, white wine Worcestershire sauce, soy sauce, red wine and lemon juice in a large glass dish and mix well.

Remove the quail from the liquid. Wrap half a piece of bacon around each quail. Arrange two quail on a skewer, alternating with mushrooms, bell peppers, onion chunks and cherry tomatoes. Repeat the process for remaining skewers. Place in sauce and refrigerate, covered, for 8 hours or more.

Grill the meat and vegetables, sprinkling with Creole seasoning, basting with marinade and turning at least once. When the bell peppers are tender, the quail will be ready to eat. Makes 24 servings.

Note: For the best-looking, most evenly cooked quail, tie or skewer the legs together before cooking. A wooden pick works well for this.

Quail-on-a-Spit

4 quail
1/2 cup (1 stick) margarine
4 slices bacon
Salt and pepper to taste

Rinse quail and drain on paper towels. Melt margarine in a skillet. Brown quail in hot margarine. Drain. Wrap each quail with bacon. Center the quail on a rotisserie spit. Grill with the lid closed for 30 to 45 minutes or to desired doneness. Season with salt and pepper before serving. Makes 4 servings.

Buttery Smoked Quail

12 quail breasts
Salt and pepper to taste
1 cup (2 sticks) melted butter
12 slices bacon

Season the quail with salt and pepper. Dip in the melted butter just before cooking. Wrap each quail breast with a strip of bacon. Secure with wooden picks. Place on a rack in a preheated water smoker with wet hickory chips added to the charcoal. Smoke for 1 hour. Check for doneness. Continue cooking until legs move easily. You may also grill, covered, for 1 hour. Makes 6 servings.

Smoked Quail in Bacon

12 quail
1 cup (2 sticks) melted margarine
Lawry's seasoned salt to taste
12 slices bacon

Brush each quail with margarine. Sprinkle with seasoned salt. Wrap each quail with a slice of bacon and secure with a wooden pick. Prepare a medium-hot charcoal fire with wet hickory chips added. Place quail on a rack and grill, covered, for 30 minutes. Check for doneness and continue cooking until legs move easily when rotated.
Makes 12 servings.

Fried Quail

4 quail
3 cups milk
1/4 cup flour
1 teaspoon salt
Dash pepper
4 cups peanut oil

Combine the quail and milk in a large bowl. Let stand for 1 hour. Drain. Coat the quail thoroughly in flour mixed with salt and pepper. Heat the oil to 350 degrees in a deep skillet over medium-high heat. Add the quail and cook, covered, for about 10 minutes or until brown on both sides, turning every 3 to 5 minutes. Drain on paper towels. Makes 4 servings.

Cross Quail and Milk Gravy

6 quail
2 cups milk
4 beef bouillon cubes
2 cups water
2 cups peanut oil
2 cups self-rising flour
1 teaspoon Lawry's seasoned salt
2 tablespoons self-rising flour

Combine the quail and milk in a large bowl and let stand for 30 to 45 minutes. Dissolve the bouillon cubes in the water in a bowl. Heat oil to 350 degrees in a deep heavy skillet. Remove the quail from the milk, reserving the milk. Coat with 2 cups flour mixed with seasoned salt. Fry in hot oil, covered, until golden brown, turning occasionally. Drain most of the oil. Add 2 tablespoons flour to the remaining oil and mix well. Cook until the flour is browned, stirring constantly. Add the bouillon and reserved milk to the skillet. Cook until thickened, stirring constantly. Makes 6 servings.

Quail Toast

24 quail
1 cup corn oil
1 quart water
6 (4-ounce) cans chopped mushrooms
1 cup dry sherry
$1^1/2$ teaspoons Kitchen Bouquet
$^1/4$ cup cornstarch
Salt and coarse ground pepper
24 slices toast

Sauté the quail in hot oil in a large skillet until lightly browned. Bring the water to a boil in a stockpot. Add the quail, mushrooms, sherry and Kitchen Bouquet. Cook for about 10 minutes or until the quail are tender Stir in the cornstarch. Cook until thickened, stirring constantly. Add salt and pepper. Serve on toast. Makes 24 servings.

Smothered Quail

6 quail
6 tablespoons butter
3 tablespoons flour
2 cups chicken broth
$^1/4$ cup dry sherry
Salt and pepper to taste

Brown the quail in hot butter in a heavy ovenproof skillet or Dutch oven. Remove and arrange in a baking dish. Add the flour to the skillet and mix well. Add the chicken broth gradually, stirring constantly. Stir in the sherry, salt and pepper. Pour over the quail. Bake, covered, at 350 degrees for 1 hour. Serve with hot cooked rice. Makes 6 servings.

Baked Quail with Ginger Orange Relish

6 quail
3 dozen peeled grapes
Juice of 1/2 lemon
Salt and pepper to taste
6 slices bacon
1/4 cup (1/2 stick) melted butter
Ginger Orange Relish (below)

Fill the cavities of the quail with the grapes. Rub the outside of the quail with lemon juice, salt and pepper. Wrap each quail with bacon. Arrange in a baking dish and drizzle with the butter. Bake, covered, at 400 degrees until tender. Serve with Ginger Orange Relish. Makes 6 servings.

Ginger Orange Relish

2 tablespoons prepared mustard
1 cup orange marmalade
1/2 teaspoon ground ginger

Combine the mustard, marmalade and ginger in a microwave-safe bowl or saucepan and microwave on High until hot. Makes about 1 cup.

Stuffed Quail

3 cups water
1 teaspoon salt
1 cup wild rice, rinsed
1/4 cup (1/2 stick) butter
1 1/2 cups sliced mushrooms
2 tablespoons chopped onion
1/3 cup (about 5 tablespoons) melted butter
8 quail
8 slices bacon

Bring the water and salt to a boil in a medium saucepan. Add the rice and cover. Boil for 20 to 25 minutes.

Melt 1/4 cup butter in a medium skillet over low heat. Add the mushrooms and onion and cook until the mushrooms are browned. Remove from the heat. Reserve 1/4 cup of the mushrooms for garnish. Combine the remaining mushrooms and onion with the wild rice and 1/3 cup melted butter in a bowl. Toss gently to mix. Stuff the rice into the cavity of the quail (you will likely have leftover rice). Wrap each quail with bacon. Place in an ungreased baking dish. Bake at 375 degrees for 1 hour. Serve with any remaining rice and reserved mushrooms. Makes 8 servings.

Baked Quail with Dressing

1 onion, diced
1/4 cup (1/2 stick) butter
4 cups bread cubes, toasted
1 (10-ounce) can cream of mushroom soup
2 eggs, beaten
Salt and pepper to taste
8 quail
8 slices bacon

Sauté the onion in hot butter in a large skillet. Add the bread cubes, soup, eggs, salt and pepper and mix well. Stuff dressing into cavity of quail. Wrap each quail with bacon. Arrange in a baking dish. Add a small amount of water. Bake at 350 degrees for 1 hour. Makes 8 servings.

Cherry Quail

6 quail
6 slices bacon
1 tablespoon butter
1 tablespoon flour
1 tablespoon cherry jelly
1 teaspoon pepper

Rinse the quail and drain on paper towels. Wrap each quail with bacon. Place the quail breast side up in a roasting pan. Roast at 350 degrees for 45 minutes. Place the quail on a warm platter, reserving the pan juices. Melt the butter in a saucepan. Add the flour and cook until the flour is browned, stirring occasionally. Add the jelly and mix well. Stir in the pan juices. Cook until the mixture is thickened, stirring constantly. Add the pepper. Pour the gravy into a gravy boat or serving bowl. Serve the quail with the gravy. Makes 6 servings.

Simmered Quail

6 tablespoons melted butter
3 tablespoons Worcestershire sauce
3 tablespoons soy sauce
Dash garlic powder
1/4 teaspoon salt
Pepper to taste
12 quail
Flour

Combine the butter, Worcestershire sauce, soy sauce, garlic powder, salt and pepper in a bowl. Dip the quail into the sauce. Coat lightly with flour. Fill a baking dish half full of water. Add the quail and cover tightly. Bake at 350 degrees for 30 minutes or until tender. Remove the cover and bake for 10 minutes longer to brown.
Makes 12 servings.

Quail Paprikash

- 3/4 cup flour
- 2 teaspoons salt
- 1/2 teaspoon pepper
- 1 teaspoon paprika
- 12 quail
- 3/4 cup (1 1/2 sticks) margarine
- 1/2 cup vegetable oil
- 1 (6-ounce) package egg noodles
- Salt to taste
- 2 garlic cloves, crushed
- 2 tablespoons margarine

Combine the flour, salt, pepper and paprika in a bag or on waxed paper or a plate. Coat the quail with the mixture.

Heat 3/4 cup margarine and oil in a large baking pan in a 350-degree oven. Place the quail in the hot margarine mixture. Bake at 350 degrees for 30 minutes, turning once. Cooking time will depend on age and tenderness of quail, so check frequently.

Cook the noodles in salted water according to package directions. Drain. Sauté the garlic cloves in 2 tablespoons margarine in a saucepan. Remove the garlic. Toss the drained noodles with the margarine. Arrange the cooked quail on a large serving platter. Pour the pan drippings over the noodles and mix well. Arrange the noodles around the quail. Makes 12 servings.

Quail in Sweet Potato

- 4 large sweet potatoes
- Vegetable oil
- 1/2 cup (1 stick) butter
- 1 tablespoon brown sugar
- 1 tablespoon ground allspice
- 4 quail
- 1/2 teaspoon Lawry's seasoned salt
- 2 cups vegetable oil
- 1/2 cup pecans, chopped

Rub the sweet potatoes with oil. Wrap in aluminum foil. Bake at 350 degrees for 1 hour or until tender. Cut the potatoes into halves crosswise. Scoop out the pulp and place in a bowl. Reserve the sweet potato shells. Add the butter, brown sugar and allspice to the sweet potato pulp and mix well.

Sprinkle the quail with seasoned salt, then brown the quail in 2 cups oil in a large skillet. Place a quail in each of the sweet potato shells. Place on a sheet of heavy-duty aluminum foil. Pat remaining sweet potato mixture over quail. Top with the pecans. Seal the foil and place in a roasting pan. Bake at 350 degrees for 1 hour.

Makes 4 servings.

Quail and Dirty Rice

8 quail
$1/2$ cup (1 stick) butter
2 cups mushrooms, sliced
$1/2$ cup sliced green onions
1 cup dry white wine
2 tablespoons lemon juice
Salt and freshly ground pepper to taste
Dirty Rice

Brown the quail in hot butter in a large skillet. Remove from the skillet, reserving drippings. Sauté the mushrooms and green onions in the skillet. Place the quail, mushrooms, green onions and wine in a baking dish. Bake, covered with aluminum foil, at 350 degrees for 1 hour, basting often with a mixture of lemon juice, salt and pepper. Remove the foil during the last 15 minutes of baking time. Serve with hot cooked Dirty Rice. Makes 6 to 8 servings.

Dirty Rice

$1\frac{1}{2}$ cups wild rice
4 (10-ounce) cans beef broth
1 cup chopped onion
1 cup chopped green bell pepper
1 cup sliced mushrooms
$1/4$ cup ($1/2$ stick) butter
1 cup heavy cream
Salt and pepper to taste

Rinse the rice. Cook in the beef broth in a saucepan according to package directions until most of the liquid is absorbed. Sauté the onion, bell pepper and mushrooms in hot butter in a skillet. Add the cream, salt and pepper and mix well. Add to cooked rice. Spoon into a baking dish. Bake at 350 degrees for 20 minutes. Makes about 6 servings.

Quail Casserole

6 quail
Salt and pepper to taste
Flour
1/2 cup vegetable oil
1/2 cup chopped onion
1/2 cup chopped green bell pepper
1 (10-ounce) can cream of celery or mushroom soup
1 soup can water
1 cup rice

Sprinkle the quail with salt and pepper. Coat with flour. Brown in hot oil in a large skillet. Remove from the skillet. Sauté the onion and bell pepper in the pan drippings. Add the soup, water and rice and mix well. Pour into a baking dish. Arrange the quail on top. Bake, covered, at 350 degrees for 45 minutes. Makes 6 servings.

Wild Birds and Mushrooms in Wine

8 to 12 quail, dove or pheasant quarters
Salt to taste
Flour
1/3 cup (5 tablespoons) butter
12 ounces fresh mushrooms, sliced
1 1/2 tablespoons parsley flakes
2 1/2 cups dry white wine

Split the quail down the back. Salt and lightly coat the quail with flour. Brown all over in hot butter in a skillet. Remove the quail from the skillet. Place in a baking dish. Pour the drippings from skillet over quail. Add the mushrooms and parsley to the dish. Pour enough wine into the dish to half cover the quail. Cover and bake at 350 degrees for 1 hour. Dove should be baked for 45 minutes, pheasant quarters for 1 hour. Makes 8 to 12 servings.

Fowl

Fowl
Fowl
Fowl
Fowl
Fowl
Fowl
Fowl
Fowl

Wild Goose with Sour Cream and Mushrooms

1 (5- to 8-pound) goose
Garlic salt and paprika to taste
1 1/2 ribs celery, chopped
1 carrot, chopped
1 onion, chopped
1/3 cup vegetable oil
1/4 cup flour
1/2 teaspoon dried rosemary
1/4 teaspoon dried thyme
1 1/4 teaspoons salt
1 cup sour cream
1 (4-ounce) can mushrooms, drained

Rinse and dry the goose inside and out. Cut off the neck and wing tips and reserve. Sprinkle the goose inside and out with garlic salt and paprika. Place on a rack in a roasting pan. Roast, uncovered, at 325 degrees for 1 hour or until golden brown and fat melts into the bottom of the pan.

Simmer the giblets, neck and wing tips in water to cover in a saucepan to make a stock. Cook the celery, carrot and onion in hot oil in a medium skillet until tender and golden brown. Add 2 tablespoons of the flour to skillet and mix well. Add 1 cup stock and mix well. Add the rosemary, thyme and salt. Stir the remaining 2 tablespoons flour into the sour cream. Stir into liquid in skillet.

Place the goose in a roasting pan. Pour the gravy and mushrooms over the goose. Roast, covered, for 2 hours longer or until tender. Makes 4 to 6 servings.

Delta Goose

1 goose
1 teaspoon salt
1 tablespoon black pepper
1/2 teaspoon red pepper
5 garlic cloves, sliced
3 onions, diced
1/2 cup vegetable oil
3 cups water

Split the goose breast lengthwise. Rub the goose with salt, black pepper and red pepper. Make small slits in the breast. Insert 4 of the garlic cloves and two-thirds of the onions into slits. Place goose on a rack in a large pot with oil and 2 cups of the water. Cover, bring to a boil and steam until meat is tender. Remove goose from pot. Bring liquid to a boil and boil down until just drippings remain. Return the goose to the pot. Brown in drippings, turning to brown all over. Remove from the pot. Add the remaining garlic and onions to the pot and cook until tender. Add the remaining 1 cup water. Cook until thickened, stirring constantly. Serve gravy over rice with goose.
Makes 4 to 6 servings.

Saucy Apple Goose

2 apples, peeled and sliced
1 wild goose
1 (16-ounce) can applesauce
3/4 cup currant jelly
1 teaspoon cinnamon
1 teaspoon nutmeg
1/2 cup corn syrup

Place the apples in the cavity of the goose. Place the goose on a rack in a roasting pan. Roast at 350 degrees for 20 minutes per pound. Combine the applesauce, jelly, cinnamon, nutmeg and corn syrup in a saucepan and mix well. Cook over low heat until the jelly is melted and mixture is well combined, stirring constantly. Reserve a portion of the baste for use as a sauce. Baste the goose frequently with the remaining mixture. Serve with the reserved sauce. Makes 4 to 6 servings.

Fruited and Stuffed Wild Goose

1 (4- to 6-pound) Canada or White Front goose
Salt and pepper to taste
1/2 cup (1 stick) butter or margarine
1/2 cup chopped onion
1 1/2 cups peeled chopped apple
3 1/2 cups soft bread crumbs
1 cup craisins (dried sweetened cranberries)
1/4 teaspoon sage
6 slices bacon
1 cup orange juice
2 tablespoons butter or margarine, melted

Sprinkle the goose inside and out with salt and pepper. Melt 1/2 cup butter in a skillet, add the onion and apple and sauté until tender. Add the bread crumbs, craisins, sage and salt and pepper and mix well. Stuff the mixture into the goose cavity. Cover the breast and legs with bacon. Combine the orange juice and 2 tablespoons melted butter in a small bowl. Roast the goose, covered, at 325 degrees for 2 1/2 hours. Uncover, increase oven temperature to 350 degrees, and roast for 30 minutes longer. Baste goose with orange juice mixture every 15 minutes during roasting time. Makes 4 servings.

Roast Duck and Wild Rice

2 ducks
2 onions, halved
1 large apple, quartered
2 ribs celery
1 bay leaf
1 teaspoon thyme
1 quart water
Salt and pepper to taste
4 slices bacon
3 tablespoons butter
4 green onions, sliced
1 bell pepper, chopped
1 (7-ounce) can sliced mushrooms, drained
1 teaspoon salt
1 cup cooked wild rice
4 slices bacon

Place the ducks, onions, apple, celery, bay leaf, thyme, water and salt and pepper to taste in a large pot. Cook, covered, over low heat until meat is cooked halfway through. Remove ducks from the liquid. Arrange 4 slices bacon in a roasting pan. Melt the butter in a skillet and sauté green onions and bell pepper until tender. Add the mushrooms, 1 teaspoon salt and rice and mix well. Stuff ducks with rice mixture. Arrange over the bacon in the prepared pan. Wrap 4 slices bacon around ducks and secure with wooden picks. Roast at 400 degrees for 30 minutes. Makes 2 to 4 servings.

Poached Wild Duck

2 tablespoons butter
2 tablespoons dry sherry
2 tablespoons tomato paste
3 tablespoons flour
1 1/2 cups chicken broth
1/2 cup dry red wine
Salt and pepper to taste
8 ounces mushrooms
1 bay leaf
2 ducks
2 cups cooked wild rice
Spiced apple rings

Combine the butter, sherry, tomato paste, flour, chicken broth, wine, salt, pepper, mushrooms and bay leaf in a large pot and mix well. Bring to a boil over medium-high heat. Add the ducks. Cook or bake, covered, over low heat (about 275 degrees) until tender. Remove the ducks from the liquid. Place on a serving platter and surround with rice and apple rings. Makes 2 to 4 servings.

Shrimp Duck

3 ducks
1 (3-ounce) bag shrimp boil
Salt and pepper to taste
3 bacon slices, cut into halves
Garlic salt to taste
1/4 cup (1/2 stick) butter or margarine
1 teaspoon lemon juice

Combine the ducks and shrimp boil in water to cover in a large pot and bring to a boil over medium-high heat. Boil for about 30 minutes or until the meat is tender. Remove the ducks from liquid. Salt and pepper the ducks. Wrap bacon over each duck breast and secure with wooden picks. Sprinkle with garlic salt. Place the ducks on a rack in a roasting pan.

Melt the butter in a saucepan over medium heat until it begins to foam. Add the lemon juice and mix well.

Bake the ducks at 350 degrees for about 15 minutes or until browned, basting often with lemon butter.

Makes 3 to 6 servings.

Wild Duck and Dressing

2 ducks
1 1/2 cups cooking sherry
1 large onion, quartered
1 rib celery
2 garlic cloves
1 tablespoon peppercorns
2 chicken bouillon cubes
1 recipe Secret Ingredient Corn Bread, crumbled (page 159)
1/2 small loaf white bread, toasted, crumbled
10 hard-cooked eggs, chopped
Additional duck stock
Salt and pepper to taste
Dash sage
Dash ginger
1 cup melted butter

Combine the ducks, sherry, onion, celery, garlic, peppercorns and bouillon cubes in a pressure cooker. Cook at 15 pounds pressure according to manufacturer's directions for 15 minutes. Reserve the cooking liquid. Cut out and reserve whole breasts. Debone the remaining meat. Combine the deboned meat, corn bread, white bread, eggs, 3 cups stock, salt, pepper, sage and ginger in a bowl and mix well. Place in a baking dish. Top with the duck breasts. Baste with the butter. Bake, covered, at 375 degrees for 30 minutes. Uncover and bake for 15 minutes.

Makes 2 to 4 servings.

Spicy Wild Duck

- 4 ducks
- 4 garlic cloves, quartered
- 2 bay leaves
- Salt and pepper to taste
- 1 bunch green onions, chopped
- 2 large onions, chopped
- 4 ribs celery, chopped
- 2 tablespoons Worcestershire sauce
- 1 teaspoon anise seeds
- 1 teaspoon dried basil
- 4 brandied peaches
- 10 ounces water
- 4 beef bouillon cubes
- 1 cup (2 sticks) butter
- 1/3 cup sifted flour
- 1 (7-ounce) can sliced mushrooms
- 1 cup burgundy wine
- 1 teaspoon Lawry's seasoned salt
- 1/2 teaspoon salt
- 1/2 teaspoon pepper

Place the ducks in a deep baking dish. Place 1 slice garlic, 1/4 bay leaf and some salt and pepper to taste on each side of each duck breast. Place a garlic slice and 1/4 bay leaf in the cavity between the duck breast and the bone. Sprinkle the green onions, onions and celery in and around ducks. Put 1/2 tablespoon Worcestershire sauce and 1/4 of the anise seeds and basil in each duck. Place 1 peach inside each duck. Arrange the remaining garlic over each duck. Pour the water over ducks. Sprinkle with salt and pepper to taste. Add the bouillon cubes to water. Bake, covered, at 400 degrees for 1 1/2 hours. Let stand until fat rises to top of drippings. Skim and discard. Discard bay leaves. Reserve pan drippings.

Melt the butter in a large saucepan over medium heat. Add the flour and cook until flour is browned and mixture is thickened, stirring occasionally. Add the undrained mushrooms, wine, reserved pan drippings, seasoned salt, salt and 1/2 teaspoon pepper. Simmer for 30 minutes. Pour over the ducks. Bake, covered, at 450 degrees for 1 hour. Add water if sauce seems too thick. Makes 4 to 6 servings.

Vicksburg Wild Ducks

- 4 mallard ducks, dressed, giblets reserved
- 4 medium onions, chopped
- 1 tablespoon pepper
- 1 tablespoon salt
- 1/2 cup vegetable oil
- 6 garlic cloves, chopped
- 4 ribs celery, chopped
- 6 green onions, sliced
- 1 pound ham, diced
- 2 pints oysters with liquid
- Salt and pepper to taste
- 1 teaspoon Tabasco sauce
- 3 tablespoons Worcestershire sauce
- 4 cups cooked rice or wild rice
- 1 cup chopped pecans
- 1 cup parsley, chopped
- 2 cups good-quality red wine
- 4 garlic cloves
- 2 cups water
- 1 cup good-quality red wine
- 8 thick slices bacon

Bring the ducks, giblets, half of the chopped onions, 1 tablespoon pepper and water to cover to a boil in a large pot. Boil for 30 minutes. Add 1 tablespoon salt during the last 10 minutes of cooking. Remove the ducks from liquid but leave the giblets and allow them to continue simmering.

Heat the oil in a Dutch oven. Add the remaining onions, 6 garlic cloves, celery and green onions. Sauté until the onions are tender. Add the chopped giblets and ham and mix well. Stir in the liquid from the oysters; simmer for 20 minutes. Season with salt and pepper to taste, Tabasco sauce and Worcestershire sauce. Add the rice, oysters, pecans, parsley and 2 cups red wine and mix well. Simmer until the oysters curl. If mixture seems thick, add a little duck broth.

Rub the ducks inside and out with additional vegetable oil. Season with salt and pepper to taste. Cut two or three slits on each side of each duck. Insert the 4 garlic cloves into slits. Lightly spoon dressing into cavity of each duck.

Place the ducks in a roasting pan. Roast, uncovered, at 450 degrees for 15 minutes. Remove from oven. Pour 2 cups water mixed with 1 cup red wine into the pan. Place 2 strips of bacon over the breast of each duck. Reduce heat to 325 degrees and roast, covered, for 1 hour. Makes 4 to 6 servings.

Oven-Bag Duck

- 2 tablespoons flour
- 1 1/2 cups orange juice
- 2 ducks
- 1 tablespoon melted butter
- Salt to taste
- 1 apple, chopped
- 1 rib celery, chopped

Place the flour in a large oven bag, close the top of the bag and shake to coat bag. Pour the orange juice into the bag and stir or shake until well mixed. Brush the ducks with butter inside and out and sprinkle with salt. Fill the cavities with apple and celery. Place the ducks in oven bag and seal bag. Make six 1/2-inch slits in the top of the bag. Place in a roasting pan. Bake at 350 degrees for 1 1/2 hours. Makes 2 to 4 servings.

Golden Duck

1 duck
1/2 teaspoon salt
1 (16-ounce) can fruit cocktail
2/3 cup diced celery
2 tablespoons butter
1 cup bread crumbs
1/4 teaspoon salt
1/3 cup pitted prunes, diced
1/3 cup blanched or toasted almonds, chopped

Sprinkle the duck with 1/2 teaspoon salt. Drain fruit cocktail, reserving 1/4 cup syrup. Sauté the celery in butter in a skillet until tender. Add the bread crumbs, 1/4 teaspoon salt, fruit cocktail, prunes, almonds and reserved fruit cocktail syrup and mix well. Fill the cavity with stuffing. Secure the neck skin to back of duck. Cover the opening of body cavity with aluminum foil and tie the legs together. Place the duck on a rack in a roasting pan. Bake at 325 degrees for 2 hours or until drumstick meat is tender. Makes 2 to 4 servings.

Delta Duck

2 ducks
1 lemon, cut into halves
1 teaspoon salt
1 teaspoon pepper
1/2 teaspoon garlic salt
1 apple, cored and chopped
1 teaspoon Worcestershire sauce
1 medium onion, chopped
1/2 cup chopped celery
6 bacon slices

Rub the ducks with lemon inside and out. Sprinkle with salt, pepper and garlic salt. Combine the apple, Worcestershire sauce, onion and celery in a bowl. Stuff mixture into cavities. Close the cavities and secure with wooden picks. Brown the ducks in a large pot. Wrap bacon slices around ducks. Place in a roasting pan. Bake breast side down at 300 degrees for about 2 1/2 hours or until tender. Makes 2 to 4 servings.

Orange Duck

1 duck
Salt and pepper to taste
1/2 cup (1 stick) margarine, melted
1/2 cup soy sauce
2 oranges
1 tablespoon orange marmalade
2 duck livers, chopped
1 tablespoon flour
1 tablespoon curaçao liqueur

Rub the duck inside and out with salt and pepper. Brush with the melted margarine and soy sauce. Grate colored zest from oranges and set aside. Slice the oranges, remove seeds and stuff duck with orange slices combined with orange marmalade.

Place the duck in a large ovenproof skillet or ovenproof pot and sear over high heat for 10 minutes. Cover and bake at 325 degrees for 1 1/2 hours, basting occasionally. Simmer the livers in salted water to cover in a saucepan until tender. Drain and reserve the duck pan juices, skimming and discarding the fat. Combine juices, orange zest, livers and their broth. Combine a small amount of broth and flour to make a paste. Stir paste into pan juice mixture. Cook until mixture is thickened, stirring constantly. Pour curaçao into a gravy boat. Add gravy and serve with duck immediately. Makes 2 servings.

Paul W. McIlhenny's Roasted Wild Duck

Roasted duck breast served rare is just as delicious as a juicy piece of rare beef steak, but you won't believe it until you try it. Have a slow-gaited butler walk with the roasting pan of ducks at a snail's pace through a hot, hot kitchen into the dining room, where it is then ready to be carved and served.

For this method of cooking, teal, canvasback, pintail and mallard are the preferred ducks. Make sure the ducks are plucked and cleaned well, leaving the skin intact. Wipe the cavity dry. Wild ducks should be aged: put them in the bottom of the refrigerator for at least 4 days. Preheat oven to 500 degrees for 15 minutes. Place the ducks breast side up on a rack in a roasting pan. Roast for 15 to 20 minutes or until skin is brown and crispy. To test for doneness, insert a steel fork into the breast meat. Juices should run red. Carefully cut out breast in one piece. The meat will be juicy and medium rare. Serve with wild muscadine or currant jelly.

Roasted Duck with Orange Sauce

4 large ducks
1 (28-ounce) package instant rice
1 pound mild bulk pork sausage
1 small onion, chopped
2 ribs celery, chopped
1 small bell pepper, chopped
1 (20-ounce) can crushed pineapple, drained
1/2 cup packed brown sugar
1/2 cup white wine
Orange Sauce
Slivered almonds

Bring the ducks and water to cover to a boil in a large pan. Boil for 35 to 40 minutes. Drain, reserving 1 cup stock to use in the Orange Sauce.

Cook the rice according to package directions and set aside. Cook the sausage in a large skillet over medium-high heat; drain. Add the onion, celery and bell pepper. Cook until the vegetables are tender, stirring occasionally. Add the rice and pineapple and mix well. Stuff the ducks, then spoon remaining dressing into a baking pan. Arrange ducks over dressing. Dissolve the brown sugar in the white wine in a small bowl. Brush over ducks. Bake the ducks at 350 degrees for 2 hours, basting occasionally. Slice and place on a platter. Top with Orange Sauce (below) and slivered almonds. Makes 4 to 6 servings.

Orange Sauce

2 cups freshly squeezed orange juice
1/4 cup cider vinegar
2 tablespoons cornstarch
1 cup reserved duck stock
1/2 cup sugar

Combine the orange juice, vinegar, cornstarch, stock and sugar in a saucepan and mix until the cornstarch dissolves. Cook over low heat until the sauce thickens, stirring constantly. Makes about 3 1/2 cups.

Southern Roast Duck

3 ducks
1 teaspoon salt
1 teaspoon pepper
Garlic salt to taste
1 cup chopped celery
1 1/2 large onions, chopped
3 garlic cloves, chopped
2 1/2 cups water
1/4 cup Worcestershire sauce
1 1/2 tablespoons dry mustard
Dash nutmeg
2 tablespoons lemon juice
2 teaspoons flour (optional)

Rub the ducks with salt, pepper and garlic salt. Place breast side down in a roasting pan. Combine the celery, onions, garlic, water, Worcestershire sauce, mustard, nutmeg and lemon juice in a large bowl and mix well. Pour over the ducks. Bake at 350 degrees for 2 1/2 hours. You may make a gravy by combining pan drippings with flour in a saucepan and cooking over medium heat until thickened, stirring constantly. Makes 3 to 5 servings.

Roasted Teal

4 teal
2 tangerines, peeled
3/4 cup port wine
1 1/2 tablespoons lemon juice
1 cup red pepper jelly
1 1/2 teaspoons flour
2 tablespoons water

Rinse the ducks inside and out and pat dry. Separate the tangerines into halves. Insert the tangerine halves into duck cavities. Place the ducks in a roasting pan. Heat the wine, lemon juice and jelly in a saucepan and cook over low heat until the jelly is melted, stirring constantly. Pour over the ducks. Bake, uncovered, at 400 degrees for 25 minutes, basting several times. Place the ducks on a serving platter and slice as desired.

Combine the flour and water in a cup to make a paste. Stir into pan drippings. Cook over medium heat until thickened, stirring constantly. Serve over Baked Wild Rice Pilaf (page 155). Makes 4 servings.

Duck in Wine

3 large ducks
1 (750-milliliter) bottle semisweet red wine
Dash salt
Black pepper to taste
Dash garlic salt
3 ribs celery
1 medium potato
1 apple
1 onion
6 slices bacon
3 tablespoons pepper jelly
3 tablespoons cornstarch

Combine the ducks, wine and water to cover in a large container. Refrigerate, covered, for 8 to 10 hours. Remove the ducks from the liquid, reserving liquid. Rub the ducks inside and out with salt, pepper and garlic salt. Chop the celery, potato, apple and onion and place in cavities. Place 2 strips of bacon across each duck breast and secure with wooden picks. Place the ducks breast side down in a Dutch oven. Add enough of the reserved liquid to come 1/4 of the way up the ducks. Bake, covered, at 300 degrees for 2 to 3 hours. Turn breast side up. Baste with some of the pepper jelly. Broil for 2 to 3 minutes. Place the ducks on a serving platter. Add the cornstarch and remaining jelly to the pan juices. Cook over low heat until thickened. Serve the sauce with ducks. Makes 3 to 5 servings.

Barbecued Duck

4 ducks
1 (28-ounce) bottle barbecue sauce
1 cup hot pepper jelly

Rinse the ducks inside and out and pat dry. Combine the barbecue sauce and jelly in a saucepan. Cook over low heat until jelly is melted, stirring constantly. Baste the ducks with barbecue mixture. Arrange on spits. Grill over a charcoal flame, basting frequently. Makes 6 servings.

Note: For a hot pepper jelly recipe, see page 151.

Chinese-Style Duck

2 onions, chopped
1 teaspoon ginger
1/2 cup vegetable oil
1 teaspoon salt
1 teaspoon Chinese 5-spice powder
1/4 cup white wine
2 teaspoons sugar
2 wild ducks
Vegetable oil
1/2 teaspoon dried orange zest
1 teaspoon caraway seeds
1/2 teaspoon anise seeds
1 teaspoon salt

Sauté the onions and ginger in 1/2 cup oil in a medium skillet. Add 1 teaspoon salt, spice powder, white wine and sugar and mix well. Stuff the cavities of ducks with mixture and close, securing with skewers.

Bring a large quantity of water to a boil in a stockpot. Place the ducks in a clean sink and pour some of the boiling water over them to seal the skin. Continue pouring water over ducks until skins cease to draw. Rub the ducks with oil. Brown in a large skillet or pot. Place the ducks in a large deep pan and add water to within 1/2 inch of top of duck. Add the orange zest, caraway seeds, anise seeds and 1 teaspoon salt to water. Bring the water to a boil. Lower heat and simmer for 3 to 4 hours. Makes 2 or 3 servings.

Mississippi Duck Stew

4 ducks
1/4 cup flour
1 teaspoon salt
1 teaspoon pepper
Dash garlic salt
Dash celery salt
3/4 cup peanut oil
1 cup chopped onion
1 cup chopped green bell pepper
1/2 cup flour
4 chicken bouillon cubes
4 cups hot water

Cut the ducks into serving pieces. Coat with the flour mixed with salt, pepper, garlic salt and celery salt. Brown in hot peanut oil in a heavy skillet. Remove from skillet. Add the onion and bell pepper to skillet. Sauté until tender, then remove from skillet. Stir the flour into oil in skillet and continue cooking until browned. Dissolve the bouillon cubes in hot water in a bowl. Add to the skillet along with duck and vegetables. Cook, covered, over medium-low heat for 1 1/2 hours. Serve with brown, white or wild rice. Makes 8 servings.

Cross Smoked Duck Breasts

6 duck breasts
1 (16-ounce) bottle Italian salad dressing
1 tablespoon Lawry's seasoned salt
6 slices bacon

Skin and debone the duck breasts. Combine the meat with Italian dressing in a bowl. Refrigerate for 4 to 6 hours. Remove the meat from dressing. Sprinkle with the seasoned salt. Wrap with bacon and secure bacon with wooden picks. Grill over a charcoal fire with wet hickory chips added for 18 to 20 minutes, turning twice.
Makes 4 servings.

Duck Tenders with Mushrooms

Breast meat of 4 large ducks
1 cup flour
Dash salt and pepper
1 teaspoon sage
1/2 cup (1 stick) butter
1 cup chopped fresh mushrooms
1 cup chopped white onion
1 cup chopped celery
3 slices bacon, crisp-fried and crumbled
1/2 teaspoon thyme
1/4 teaspoon garlic salt
1/4 cup (1/2 stick) butter

Cut the duck meat into strips. Coat with a mixture of flour, salt, pepper and sage. Brown in 1/2 cup hot butter in a heavy skillet over medium heat. Remove the meat. Add the mushrooms, onion and celery to skillet. Cook until tender, stirring occasionally. Add the duck, bacon, thyme, garlic salt and 1/4 cup butter to skillet. Simmer for 30 minutes, stirring frequently. Serve over hot cooked rice.
Makes 6 servings.

Slow-Baked Duck Casserole

6 duck breasts
1/2 cup milk
1 egg
1 teaspoon garlic salt
Dash cayenne pepper
Dash salt
1 cup self-rising flour
1 cup peanut oil
1/4 cup (1/2 stick) butter
1 (10-ounce) can cream of mushroom soup
1 cup water

Cut the duck breasts into quarters. Combine the milk, egg, garlic salt, cayenne pepper and salt in a bowl. Dip the duck into the mixture, then coat with flour. Heat the oil and butter in a large heavy skillet to 375 degrees. Fry the meat in hot oil mixture until golden brown. Place the meat in a single layer in a baking dish. Combine the soup and water in a bowl and mix well. Pour over the meat. Bake, covered, at 250 degrees for 3 hours. Increase the oven temperature to 300 degrees and bake for 30 minutes longer. Makes 8 servings.

Duck Breasts in Wok

4 duck breasts
2 cups red wine
1 tablespoon cornstarch
2 tablespoons peanut oil
1 bell pepper, cut into strips
1 onion, thinly sliced
3 ribs celery, thinly sliced on the diagonal
1 (8-ounce) can water chestnuts, drained, sliced
1 teaspoon salt
Dash pepper

Skin the duck breasts and cut the meat into thin strips. Combine with the red wine and cornstarch in a bowl and mix well. Let stand for 30 minutes.

Heat the peanut oil in a wok or large skillet. Remove the meat from marinade and place in wok. Stir-fry until the meat is seared all over. Add the bell pepper, onion, celery and water chestnuts to wok and mix well. Cook, covered, over medium-high heat for 5 minutes, stirring occasionally. Season with salt and pepper. Serve over chow mein noodles or hot cooked rice.
Makes 4 to 6 servings.

Duck in Sweet-and-Sour Sauce

- 2 duck breasts, cut into cubes
- 1/4 cup sherry
- 1/4 cup soy sauce
- 3 eggs, beaten
- 1 cup flour
- 3 cups vegetable oil
- Sweet-and-Sour Sauce (below)

Combine the duck, sherry and soy sauce in a bowl. Refrigerate for 30 minutes. Drain. Dip the meat into beaten eggs, then roll in flour to coat. Fry in 350-degree oil in a skillet for 4 to 5 minutes. Combine the cooked meat with Sweet-and-Sour Sauce. Serve with hot cooked rice.
Makes 4 to 6 servings.

Sweet-and-Sour Sauce

- 1 tablespoon cornstarch
- 1 (20-ounce) can juice-pack pineapple chunks
- 1 cup water
- 2 tablespoons vinegar
- 1/3 cup packed brown sugar
- 1 (4-ounce) jar baby food apricots
- 1 tablespoon soy sauce
- 2 garlic cloves, minced
- 1 white onion, sliced thin
- 1 tomato, cut into wedges
- 1/2 cup maraschino cherries
- 1/2 cup maraschino cherry juice
- 1/4 teaspoon ginger
- 1 tablespoon sherry
- 1/4 to 1/2 teaspoon salt
- 1 bell pepper, cut into chunks
- 3/4 cup sweet pickle mix

Combine the cornstarch with a small amount of juice from the pineapples in a medium saucepan. Stir to form a paste. Add remaining juice and water. Cook over low heat until clear and thickened, stirring constantly. Add the vinegar, brown sugar, apricots, soy sauce, garlic, onion, tomato, cherries, cherry juice, ginger, sherry, salt, bell pepper and pickles and mix well. Simmer for 5 minutes.
Makes about 6 cups.

Marinated Duck Legs

12 to 18 duck thighs
1/2 teaspoon salt
1/3 teaspoon lemon pepper
1 cup ketchup
1/3 cup honey
1/4 cup lemon juice

Skin and rinse the duck thighs. Sprinkle with the salt and lemon pepper and place in a large container. Combine the ketchup, honey and lemon juice in a bowl and pour over meat. Refrigerate for 6 to 8 hours. Remove from the marinade and place in a baking pan. Bake at 250 degrees for 1 hour or until golden brown. Makes 8 to 10 servings.

Duck and Rice Casserole

2 large ducks, dressed
3 ribs celery, cut into chunks
1 onion, halved
1 1/2 teaspoons salt
1/4 teaspoon pepper
1 (4-ounce) can sliced mushrooms
1/4 cup chopped onion
1/2 cup (1 stick) margarine
1/4 cup flour
1 1/2 cups half-and-half
1 (6-ounce) package long grain and wild rice mix, cooked according to package directions
1 tablespoon chopped parsley
1/2 cup slivered almonds

Combine the ducks, celery, onion halves, salt, pepper and water to cover in a large pot and simmer for about 1 hour or until ducks are tender. Remove the ducks, reserving stock. Debone the meat and cut into bite-size pieces. Drain the mushrooms, reserving liquid. Strain the duck stock and add enough to mushroom liquid to measure 1 1/2 cups.

Sauté 1/4 cup onion in margarine in a skillet over medium heat until tender. Add the flour, mushrooms and half-and-half. Cook for 1 minute, stirring constantly. Stir in the stock mixture gradually and cook until thickened, stirring constantly. Add the duck, rice and parsley and mix well. Spoon into a 2-quart baking dish and sprinkle with the almonds. Bake, covered, at 350 degrees for about 15 to 20 minutes or until hot. Uncover and cook for 6 to 8 minutes longer to brown the almonds.
Makes 6 to 8 servings.

Duck Spread

3 ducks, dressed
2 bay leaves
Dash red pepper
Dash black pepper
Dash salt
2 cups mayonnaise
2 onions, finely chopped
1 rib celery, finely chopped
1 teaspoon chili powder
2 hard-cooked eggs, chopped

Combine the ducks, bay leaves, red pepper, black pepper, salt and water to cover in a pot or pressure cooker. Boil or pressure cook until the ducks are tender. Remove the ducks from the liquid. Skin, debone, and finely chop or grind. Combine the duck, mayonnaise, onions, celery, chili powder and eggs in a large bowl and mix well. Serve with crackers or use as a sandwich spread. Makes 2 to 4 cups.

Cheesy Crumb-Topped Duck Casserole

2 1/2 cups diced cooked duck
1 1/2 cups shredded Cheddar cheese
5 cups chicken broth
1 1/2 cups chopped onion
1 1/2 cups chopped celery
1/2 teaspoon pepper
1/2 teaspoon salt
1 (10-ounce) can cream of mushroom soup
4 cups butter cracker crumbs

Combine the duck, cheese, broth, onion, celery, pepper, salt, soup and 3 cups of the cracker crumbs in a large bowl and mix well. Spoon into a 9x13-inch baking dish. Sprinkle with the remaining 1 cup cracker crumbs. Bake at 350 degrees for 45 minutes. Make 4 to 6 servings.

Duck Soup

4 duck breasts
1 (10-ounce) can cream of celery soup
2 (10-ounce) cans cream of mushroom soup
1/2 teaspoon salt
1 teaspoon pepper
1 1/2 cups milk

Quarter each duck breast. Boil the duck in water to cover in a large pot for 10 minutes. Drain. Combine the soups, salt, pepper and milk in a separate pot. Add meat and mix well. Simmer for 20 minutes, stirring occasionally. Serve with hot cooked rice. Makes 4 to 6 servings.

Duck Gumbo

1 cup vegetable oil
1 cup flour
1 rib celery, finely chopped
6 garlic cloves, chopped
8 onions, finely chopped
3 bell peppers, chopped
3 quarts water or stock
6 to 8 ducks, cooked, skinned and deboned
1 (10-ounce) can diced tomatoes and green chiles
2 ounces Kitchen Bouquet
1/2 teaspoon thyme
1/2 teaspoon ground oregano
1 bay leaf
1 (10-ounce) package frozen okra
2 tablespoons salt
1 tablespoon pepper

Heat oil in a large flat-bottom pan. Add the flour and cook until chocolate brown, stirring constantly. Add the celery, garlic, onions and bell peppers to pan. Cook until vegetables are tender, stirring often. Add the water, duck, tomatoes, Kitchen Bouquet, thyme, oregano and bay leaf and simmer over very low heat for 1 hour. Do not allow mixture to boil. Add the okra, salt and pepper after 30 minutes. Remove bay leaf before serving.
Makes 8 to 10 servings.

Variation: For seafood gumbo, add 5 pounds of peeled shrimp and 6 small cans of crab claw meat 20 minutes before end of cooking period.

Notes: To get the best-tasting duck meat for this recipe, boil ducks in water to cover with a bay leaf.

If you achieve a dark brown roux for this recipe, you may eliminate the Kitchen Bouquet, which is primarily used to give foods an attractive brown color.

Duck and Sausage Gumbo

- 3/4 cup crumbled bacon
- 1 cup diced onions
- 1/4 cup flour
- 1/4 cup peanut oil
- 1 quart hot water
- 1 teaspoon seasoned salt
- 1 cup sliced green onions
- 1 cup parsley, chopped
- 1 tablespoon chili powder
- 1 teaspoon dry mustard
- 1 teaspoon white pepper
- 1/2 teaspoon Chowchow (page 150) or pepper relish
- 1 large duck or 2 small ducks, dressed
- 1 pound smoked link sausage
- 1 (16-ounce) can tomatoes (optional)
- 1 (4-ounce) can shrimp or oysters

Sauté the bacon, onions and flour in peanut oil in a pot over medium heat until tender. Add the hot water, seasoned salt, green onions, parsley, chili powder, dry mustard, white pepper and chowchow and mix well. Add the duck. Simmer for 1 hour. Remove the duck from the liquid. Debone and cut the meat into bite-size pieces. Return the meat to the pot. Cut the sausage into small pieces and add to the pot along with the tomatoes and shrimp. Simmer for 1 hour longer. Serve over hot cooked rice. Makes 4 to 6 servings.

Duck Jambalaya

1 duck, dressed and cut into quarters
2 teaspoons salt
1/2 teaspoon pepper
1/2 cup shortening
2 cups chicken broth
1/3 cup dried onion flakes
1/4 cup dried bell pepper flakes
1/4 teaspoon instant minced garlic
1/4 cup water
1/2 pound bulk pork sausage
1 cup rice
1 bay leaf
1/2 teaspoon chili powder
1/2 teaspoon thyme
1 teaspoon parsley flakes
1/2 cup diced cooked ham
1 cup canned whole tomatoes

Rub the duck with salt and pepper. Brown in hot shortening in a Dutch oven or other heavy pot over medium heat. Pour off the pan drippings. Add the broth to the pot. Cover and simmer over low heat for 1 1/2 hours or until the meat is tender. Combine the onion flakes, bell pepper flakes, garlic and water in a bowl and let stand. Brown the sausage in a skillet. Drain. Add rice and rehydrated vegetables. Cook, uncovered, until rice begins to stick, stirring constantly.

Remove the duck from the pot. Add the rice mixture to broth in pot and mix well. Add the bay leaf, chili powder, thyme and parsley flakes and mix well. Cook, covered, for 10 minutes. Add the ham and tomatoes and mix gently. Place the duck on top of mixture. Cook, covered, for 10 minutes longer. Remove the bay leaf before serving. Makes 4 to 6 servings.

Morgan City Coot

- 2 coot
- Salt to taste
- 2 onions, chopped
- 1/4 cup (1/2 stick) butter
- 1/2 teaspoon salt
- 1/2 teaspoon pepper
- 1/4 teaspoon allspice
- 1/2 teaspoon caraway seeds
- 1/2 cup heavy cream or half-and-half
- 1/2 cup flour

Remove all the fat from the coot. Soak in salted water to cover in a pot for at least 8 hours. Drain and rinse well. Debone and chop the meat.

Sauté the onions in butter in a large skillet. Add the meat and cook until browned. Add 1/2 teaspoon salt, pepper, allspice and caraway seeds and mix well. Add water to cover. Cook until the meat is tender. Stir a little cream into flour in a bowl to make a paste. Add the remaining cream and mix until smooth. Stir into the liquid in the skillet. Bring to a boil and boil for 1 1/2 minutes or until thickened, stirring constantly. Makes 4 servings.

Dove with Wine

- 12 dove
- Flour
- Salt and pepper to taste
- 1/2 cup vegetable oil
- 1/2 cup water
- 1 (10-ounce) can cream of mushroom soup
- 1/2 cup chopped celery
- 1/2 cup red wine

Roll the dove in flour seasoned with salt and pepper. Brown in hot oil in a large skillet. Drain off the drippings. Place the dove in a 2-quart baking dish. Combine the water, soup, celery and wine in a bowl and mix well. Pour over the dove. Bake, covered, at 350 degrees for 45 minutes. Makes 4 to 6 servings.

Roast Dove

10 dove
2 teaspoons baking soda
1 tablespoon salt
Salt and pepper to taste
Flour
1/4 cup (1/2 stick) butter

Combine the dove, baking soda and 1 tablespoon salt in a bowl. Refrigerate for 8 hours. Drain. Combine the dove and 1 inch water in a pressure cooker. Cook for 10 minutes according to manufacturer's directions. Remove the dove from the liquid and place breast side up in a baking dish. Measure the liquid from the cooker and add enough water to measure 3 cups. Pour over dove. Sprinkle with salt, pepper and flour and dot with butter. Bake at 350 degrees for about 20 minutes or until the meat is lightly browned, basting every 5 minutes. Serve with hot cooked rice. Makes 4 servings.

Baked Dove

8 dove
Flour
Salt and pepper to taste
Vegetable oil
1 (10-ounce) can beef consommé
1 teaspoon Worcestershire sauce
1 teaspoon onion juice
1/2 cup sherry plus more for basting

Coat the dove in flour mixed with salt and pepper. Brown in hot oil in a skillet. Remove and place in a roasting pan or Dutch oven.

Pour the consommé into the skillet. Cook over medium-low heat until thickened, stirring frequently. Add the Worcestershire sauce and onion juice and mix well. Pour over dove. Drizzle with the sherry. Bake at 250 degrees for 30 minutes, basting occasionally with water and wine. Makes 4 servings.

Barbecued Dove

6 dove
1/2 teaspoon salt
1/4 teaspoon pepper
1/4 teaspoon MSG
1 cup (2 sticks) margarine
Juice and zest of 6 lemons
5 ounces steak sauce
5 ounces Worcestershire sauce
1/2 teaspoon salt
1/4 teaspoon pepper
Dash MSG

Rub the dove with 1/2 teaspoon salt, 1/4 teaspoon pepper and 1/4 teaspoon MSG. Place in a roasting pan with a very small amount of water in the bottom. Roast at 450 degrees until browned.

Melt margarine in a large saucepan. Add the lemon juice and zest, steak sauce, Worcestershire sauce, 1/2 teaspoon salt, pepper and dash of MSG and mix well. Pour over the dove. Reduce the oven temperature to 350 degrees and bake, covered, for 1 hour, basting 3 or 4 times.
Makes 2 or 3 servings.

Dove Casserole

2 cups rice
1 envelope onion soup mix
2 (4-ounce) cans mushrooms, drained, or 8 ounces fresh mushrooms, sliced
2 (14-ounce) cans chicken broth
12 dove

Combine the rice, soup mix and mushrooms in a large bowl and mix well. Add the broth and mix well. Spoon into a baking dish. Arrange the dove over the rice mixture. Bake, covered, at 275 degrees for 2 hours, adding more broth or water if the mixture seems dry.
Makes 4 to 6 servings.

Braised Dove Supreme

12 dove breasts
1 cup flour for coating
1 cup vegetable oil
2 (10-ounce) cans beef consommé
1 carrot, minced
1 onion, minced
3 ribs celery, chopped
1/4 cup cooking sherry

Coat the dove with flour. Brown in hot oil in a large ovenproof skillet. Remove dove and drain excess oil from skillet. Add the consommé, carrot, onion, celery and sherry and cook until slightly thickened, stirring frequently. Add the dove and bake at 325 degrees for 1 hour. Serve with brown rice pilaf. Makes 4 to 6 servings.

Sausage Dove

1 pound smoked link sausage
2 garlic cloves
1 onion, sliced
1 tablespoon vegetable oil
3 tablespoons Worcestershire sauce
1 tablespoon soy sauce
1 teaspoon salt
1/2 teaspoon white pepper
2 cups water
24 dove breasts

Brown the sausage with garlic and onion in oil in a heavy ovenproof skillet until vegetables are tender. Drain. Add the Worcestershire sauce, soy sauce, salt, pepper and water and mix well. Add the dove and baste with pan liquids. Bake, covered, at 300 degrees for 2 hours, basting every 30 minutes and adding water if the mixture seems dry. Makes 8 to 10 servings.

Dove Kabobs

12 dove
1 (8-ounce) bottle Italian salad dressing
2 large onions
2 large green bell peppers
1 pint cherry tomatoes
1 pound sliced bacon

Combine the dove and Italian dressing in a large container. Refrigerate for at least 2 hours. Cut the onions and bell peppers into 1-inch squares. Cut the cherry tomatoes into halves. Cut the bacon into 1$^{1}/_{2}$-inch lengths

Arrange the ingredients in alternating fashion on skewers, making sure that a piece of bacon is on both sides of each dove. Grill over medium heat until meat is cooked through, turning occasionally.
Makes 4 to 6 servings.

Dove Breasts on the Grill

12 dove breasts
2 cups dry red wine
6 green onions, sliced
$^{1}/_{2}$ cup (1 stick) margarine
6 bacon slices, cut into halves
Lawry's seasoned salt to taste

Combine the dove and red wine in a large container and let stand for 1 hour. Stuff the green onions and 1 small pat of margarine into each breast cavity and secure by wrapping with a strip of bacon. Fasten with a wooden pick. Sprinkle with seasoned salt. Place on a large sheet of aluminum foil. Close foil. Grill for 30 minutes over medium coals or flame. Makes 4 to 6 servings.

Dove Hollandale

1 cup (2 sticks) butter
1 garlic clove, chopped
5 medium onions, chopped
4 ribs celery, chopped
4 shallots, chopped
1/2 bunch fresh parsley, chopped
14 to 16 dove
Salt, black pepper and cayenne pepper to taste
7 or 8 bacon slices, cut into halves
2 (7-ounce) cans sliced mushrooms
1 (10-ounce) can beef consommé
1 bay leaf
3 tablespoons flour

Melt the butter in a large pot over low heat. Add the garlic, onions, celery, shallots and parsley and mix well. Let simmer over low heat. Sprinkle the dove with salt, black pepper and cayenne pepper. Stuff each dove with 1/2 bacon slice. Add dove to pot. Add the undrained mushrooms, consommé and bay leaf. Cook, covered, for 1 1/2 hours. Taste and adjust seasonings.

Stir a small amount of cooking liquid into the flour in a bowl to make a smooth paste. Add to liquid in pot. Cook until the mixture thickens, stirring constantly. Remove bay leaf before serving. Serve with wild or white rice. Makes 6 to 8 servings.

Slow-Cooker Dove

6 dove
1 cup self-rising flour
Dash salt
Dash pepper
1 1/2 cups vegetable oil
1 onion, chopped
1/2 green bell pepper, chopped
2 cups water
1 (10-ounce) can cream of celery soup
1 (10-ounce) can cream of mushroom soup

Coat the dove with the flour mixed with salt and pepper. Brown in hot oil in a large skillet. Remove from the skillet and place in a slow cooker with the onion, bell pepper, water and soups. Cook on low for 6 to 8 hours. Serve over rice or toast. Makes 4 servings.

Lemony Dove

3/4 cup (1 1/2 sticks) margarine
Juice of 2 lemons
1 (10-ounce) bottle Worcestershire sauce
Salt and pepper to taste
12 dove

Melt the margarine in a large deep skillet or Dutch oven over medium-high heat. Add the lemon juice and Worcestershire sauce and mix well. Heat the mixture until very hot. Add the dove and brown them in this mixture. Reduce heat to low and simmer, uncovered, for 1 hour. Add salt and pepper. To serve, spoon cooking liquid over hot cooked rice and top with dove. Makes 4 to 6 servings.

Gin Dove Sauté

6 dove
1/2 cup flour
Salt and pepper to taste
1/2 cup (1 stick) butter
1/2 cup gin

Coat the dove with flour mixed with salt and pepper. Brown in hot butter in a skillet. Pour the gin into skillet. Simmer, covered, for 1 hour. Makes 2 or 3 servings.

Pheasant Normandy

2 thin slices salt pork
1 pheasant
2 tablespoons butter
6 apples, peeled, cored and sliced
1/2 cup sour cream
1 teaspoon salt
1/4 teaspoon pepper
1/3 cup Calvados or other apple brandy

Place the salt pork on the pheasant breast. Secure with kitchen twine. Heat the butter in a Dutch oven or flameproof metal casserole over medium-high heat. Brown the pheasant all over in the butter. Cover and simmer over medium-low heat for 15 minutes. Add the apples, sour cream, salt and pepper to pan. Stir in the Calvados. Heat, but do not allow to boil. Simmer, covered, for 30 minutes or until meat is fork tender. Remove and discard string. Serve hot with long grain and wild rice mixture and a green vegetable. Makes 2 to 4 servings.

Pheasant Breast Casserole

- 4 pheasant breasts, cut into halves
- Dash salt
- Dash pepper
- 1/4 cup (1/2 stick) margarine
- 1 (10-ounce) can cream of mushroom soup
- 1 (10-ounce) can cream of chicken soup
- 1 cup milk
- 1 onion, sliced into rings

Combine the pheasant, salt, pepper, margarine and enough water to cover in a large pot. Bring to a boil and boil for 1 hour. Place pheasant in a baking dish. Combine the soups with milk in a bowl and pour over meat. Top with onion slices. Bake, covered, at 325 degrees for 1 1/2 hours. Makes 4 to 6 servings.

Cross Pheasant and Rice Bake

- 1 cup wild rice
- 1 cup long grain rice
- 1/4 cup (1/2 stick) butter
- 2 onions, chopped
- 1 cup chopped celery
- 1 green bell pepper, chopped
- 1 pheasant breast
- 1/4 cup (1/2 stick) butter
- 1 pound diced cooked ham
- 1 (4-ounce) jar diced pimentos
- 1 teaspoon poultry seasoning
- 1 (14-ounce) can chicken broth
- Salt and pepper to taste

Rinse the wild rice. Cook according to package directions. Cook long grain rice according to package directions.

Heat 1/4 cup butter in a skillet. Add the onions, celery and bell pepper and cook until onions are tender.

Cut the pheasant into long, thin strips and sauté in 1/4 cup butter in a separate skillet. Combine the meat, onion mixture, rices, ham, pimentos, poultry seasoning, chicken broth and salt and pepper in a bowl and mix well. Spoon into a baking dish. Bake, covered, at 350 degrees for 30 minutes. Makes 2 to 4 servings.

Creamy Baked Pheasant

2 pheasant
Salt, pepper and poultry seasoning to taste
1 cup self-rising flour
1 cup vegetable oil
1/2 cup (1 stick) margarine
1 (10-ounce) bottle Heinz 57 steak sauce
1 cup heavy cream
1 large onion, chopped
8 ounces fresh mushrooms, sliced
Chopped green bell peppers

Debone the pheasant. Season with salt, pepper and poultry seasoning. Coat with flour. Brown in hot oil in a skillet. Remove from the skillet.

Melt the margarine in a saucepan. Add the steak sauce and mix well. Add the cream and mix well.

Layer the onion, mushrooms and meat in a baking dish. Pour three-fourths of the sauce over the layers. Bake, covered, at 350 degrees for 1 1/2 hours. Sprinkle chopped bell peppers over mixture. Bake uncovered for 10 minutes. Pour remaining sauce over casserole and serve. Makes 2 to 4 servings.

Smoked Pheasant Breasts in Pepper Jelly

2 pheasant breasts
2 cups milk
4 bacon slices
1 cup pepper jelly
4 beef bouillon cubes

Combine the pheasant and milk in a large bowl and refrigerate for 30 to 45 minutes. Fry the bacon in a skillet, reserving drippings. Remove the meat from the milk and coat with bacon drippings and pepper jelly. Start a charcoal fire in a water smoker. Add water and the bouillon cubes to water pan. Place wet hickory chips on the fire. Place the meat on racks and smoke for 1 1/2 hours, basting twice with pepper jelly. Slice and serve. (For a hot pepper jelly recipe, see page 151.) Makes 2 to 4 servings.

Pheasant Soup

1 pheasant
5 tablespoons butter
Salt to taste
1 (4-ounce) can mushrooms
1 1/2 quarts chicken broth
1/4 cup flour
1 (15-ounce) can artichoke hearts, drained and puréed
1 1/2 quarts chicken broth
1/3 cup soy sauce
1 (4-ounce) can mushrooms
Paprika to taste
1/2 cup sherry

Debone the pheasant, reserving and chopping the giblets. Cut the meat into thin strips and brown in 2 tablespoons of the butter in a pot. Add water to cover and salt to taste. Simmer over low heat for about 35 minutes or until half cooked. Add the undrained mushrooms and 1 1/2 quarts chicken broth. Reduce heat and simmer for 1 1/2 hours.

Brown the reserved giblets in 1 tablespoon of the butter in a saucepan. Add cold water to cover and salt to taste. Simmer over low heat for 45 minutes. Strain and discard the solids, reserving the cooking liquid.

Heat the remaining 2 tablespoons butter in a soup pot. Add the flour and cook over low heat until brown, stirring often. Add the artichoke heart purée, liquids in which pheasant and giblets were cooked and 1 1/2 quarts chicken broth. Stir in the soy sauce and simmer for a few minutes. Add the pheasant, remaining mushrooms, salt to taste, paprika and sherry. Simmer for 10 minutes longer.
Makes 10 servings.

Baked Pigeon

4 pigeons
1/2 teaspoon salt
1/2 teaspoon pepper
2 teaspoons vegetable oil
1/4 cup (1/2 stick) melted butter
1 (10-ounce) can cream of mushroom soup

Cut the pigeons into halves. Season with salt and pepper. Coat with the oil and place in a baking dish. Bake at 300 degrees for 1 hour, basting with the melted butter. When the meat is cooked through, pour the soup over the top and bake for 30 to 45 minutes longer.
Makes 2 servings.

Breast of Crow

4 crow breasts
1 tablespoon vegetable oil
Salt and pepper to taste
1 (10-ounce) can cream of mushroom soup
4 ounces Cheddar cheese, sliced

Place the crow in an oiled baking dish and sprinkle with salt and pepper. Spread the soup over the top. Bake, covered, at 325 degrees for 45 minutes. Remove from oven and place a 1-ounce slice of cheese over each breast. Return to the oven and heat for about 3 minutes or until cheese is melted. Serve hot. Makes 2 servings.

Smothered Squab

1 onion, chopped
4 green onions, sliced
3 ribs celery, chopped
1 green bell pepper, chopped
5 bacon slices, chopped
6 squab, cut into halves
1 teaspoon salt
1 teaspoon pepper
1/2 teaspoon paprika
1 tablespoon vegetable oil
1 quart water

Sauté the onion, green onions, celery, bell pepper and bacon in a skillet until onion is tender. Season the squab with salt, pepper and paprika. Sear the squab all over in hot oil in another skillet. Place in a large pan. Add the vegetable mixture and water and mix well. Cook, covered, over low heat until meat is tender. Makes 3 servings.

Mushroom Woodcock

4 woodcock breasts
1/2 teaspoon salt
1/2 teaspoon pepper
4 bacon slices
1 (4-ounce) can sliced mushrooms
3/4 cup (1 1/2 sticks) butter, melted

Sprinkle the woodcock with salt and pepper. Wrap the bacon slices around each breast and secure with a wooden pick. Place in a broiler pan with the drained mushrooms. Broil for 18 to 20 minutes or until meat is tender and cooked through, basting often with the melted butter. Makes 2 servings.

Stuffed Woodcock

4 woodcocks, giblets reserved
Salt and pepper to taste
3/4 teaspoon poultry seasoning
1/3 cup Cognac, warmed
1 egg yolk
1/2 cup fine bread crumbs
4 bacon slices
1/2 cup (1 stick) butter, melted
1 cup chicken broth
Watercress for garnish

Grind the woodcock livers, gizzards and hearts in a meat grinder or food processor. Add salt, pepper, poultry seasoning, 2 tablespoons of the Cognac, egg yolk and enough bread crumbs to make a light, moist stuffing. Mix well. Stuff the mixture into birds. Wrap the bacon around birds to enclose stuffing. Secure with wooden picks. Place birds in an ovenproof skillet or flameproof metal casserole and bake at 450 degrees for 5 minutes. Reduce the oven temperature to 325 degrees and roast for 20 minutes longer, basting frequently with melted butter. Remove from the oven when fully cooked. Heat the remaining Cognac in a small saucepan, pour over birds and ignite carefully. Shake the skillet until the flames die. Add the chicken broth to the skillet. Heat through and serve garnished with the watercress. Makes 2 servings.

Fish

Fish
Fish
Fish
Fish
Fish
Fish
Fish
Fish

Bass Amandine

1/2 cup thinly sliced almonds
1 tablespoon margarine
4 to 6 bass fillets
3 cups milk
1 teaspoon dry mustard
1 cup flour
Salt and pepper to taste
1 cup (2 sticks) margarine

Toast the almonds in 1 tablespoon margarine in a skillet over medium-high heat, watching carefully to prevent burning. Set aside.

Combine the fish, milk and mustard in a bowl and let stand for 10 minutes. Remove the fish from the milk mixture. Coat with a mixture of flour, salt and pepper. Fry in 1 cup hot margarine in a large skillet until browned all over, turning once. Drain on paper towels. Spoon the almonds over the fish to serve. Makes 4 to 6 servings.

Steamed Bass with Cheese Sauce

1 (1- to 3-pound) bass, scaled and drawn
2 cups water
1 tablespoon lemon juice
Lawry's seasoned salt to taste
Cheese Sauce (below)

Leave the head on the bass but remove the gills. Combine the water, lemon juice and seasoned salt in a fish poacher. Place the fish on a rack over, not in, water. Cover tightly and bring to a boil. Steam for 8 to 10 minutes or until the dorsal fins can be removed easily. Spoon the Cheese Sauce over the fish to serve. Makes 1 or 2 servings.

Cheese Sauce

1 1/2 tablespoons margarine
3 tablespoons chopped green bell pepper
1 tablespoon flour
Salt and pepper to taste
1 cup milk
1/4 cup shredded Cheddar cheese

Heat the margarine in a skillet or saucepan. Sauté the bell pepper in the hot margarine until tender. Stir in the flour, salt and pepper. Add the milk. Cook until the mixture thickens, stirring constantly. Add the cheese and cook until it is melted, stirring constantly. Makes 1 1/2 cups.

Pickled Bass

3 pounds bass fillets
1 gallon water
2 cups pickling salt
2 onions, sliced into rings
1 cup white port wine
1 quart white vinegar
1 tablespoon mixed pickling spices
1/2 cup sugar

Cut the fish into 1-inch cubes. Soak in the water combined with pickling salt in a large container for 12 to 24 hours. Remove and rinse in cold water. Pack the fish into clean glass pint jars alternately with the onion rings. Combine the wine, vinegar, pickling spices and sugar in a saucepan and heat until hot. Pour over the fish. Refrigerate, covered, for 3 days. Makes 6 to 8 servings.

Stuffing for Bass

1 cup finely chopped onions
1/2 bell pepper, finely chopped
6 tablespoons margarine
2 cups corn bread crumbs
1 cup "Contraband Crab Meat" (page 126)
1/2 cup green onion tops, chopped
Garlic salt, salt and pepper to taste

Sauté the onions and bell pepper in the margarine in a large skillet until tender. Stir in the corn bread crumbs, "Contraband Crab Meat," green onions, garlic salt, salt and pepper. Use this mixture to stuff 2 large or 4 to 6 small bass. Bake stuffed fish at 350 degrees for 40 minutes. Makes about 4 cups.

Baked Bass

1 tablespoon salt
Juice of 1 lemon
1 (4- to 5-pound) bass, scaled and drawn
2 cups bread crumbs
1 (4-ounce) can mushrooms, drained
1 onion, diced
1 tablespoon chopped celery
1/4 cup (1/2 stick) butter, melted
Dash thyme
Pepper to taste
1 tablespoon brandy
1 tablespoon heavy cream

Combine the salt and lemon juice in a small bowl. Rub the fish inside and out with the mixture. Combine the bread crumbs, mushrooms, onion, celery and butter in a bowl. Stir in the thyme, pepper, brandy and cream and mix well. Pour over the fish in a baking dish. Bake at 350 degrees for 45 minutes. Makes 3 servings.

Cross Battered Bass

1 1/2 cups baking mix
1 teaspoon sugar
1 teaspoon garlic salt
Dash salt
Dash pepper
1 1/2 cups beer
5 bass fillets, cut into strips
1 cup self-rising flour
2 cups peanut oil

Combine the baking mix, sugar, garlic salt, salt, pepper and beer in a bowl. Coat the fish with the flour, then dip into the batter. Fry in hot peanut oil in a heavy skillet until golden brown. Drain on paper towels. Serve hot.
Makes 4 to 6 servings.

Bass Chowder

6 medium bass fillets
8 ounces salt pork, diced
3 large carrots, peeled and diced
3 medium white onions, diced
1 medium green bell pepper, diced
2 tablespoons chopped parsley
1/4 cup (1/2 stick) margarine
1 (14-ounce) can whole tomatoes
3 medium potatoes, peeled and cubed
1/3 teaspoon thyme
2 small bay leaves
1/2 teaspoon pepper
Salt to taste

Combine the bass and water to cover (about 1 quart) in a soup pot and bring to a boil. Boil until the fish flakes easily. Remove the fish from the cooking liquid and flake into small pieces. Reserve the liquid.

Fry the salt pork in a soup pot over medium heat for about 3 minutes; drain. Add the carrots, onions, bell pepper, parsley and margarine. Fry for about 5 minutes. Drain the tomatoes, reserving juice. Add the tomatoes to the soup pot. Add fish to soup pot. Combine reserved tomato juice and fish cooking liquid and add to soup pot. Add the potatoes, thyme, bay leaves and pepper to soup pot. Simmer for 40 minutes. Add salt. Remove the bay leaves before serving. Makes 6 to 8 servings.

Buttermilk Bream

3 cups flour
1 teaspoon salt
2 teaspoons pepper
2 eggs
1 quart buttermilk
Juice of 1 lemon
12 bream or bream fillets
Vegetable oil for frying

Combine the flour, salt, pepper, eggs, buttermilk and lemon juice in a large bowl and mix well. Place the fish in the mixture and let stand for 20 minutes. Fry in hot oil in a skillet until brown. Makes 10 to 15 servings.

Smoky Broiled Bream

1 cup (2 sticks) margarine
$1/2$ teaspoon onion salt
$1/2$ teaspoon garlic salt
1 teaspoon pepper
$1/2$ teaspoon Worcestershire sauce
1 teaspoon vinegar
1 large onion, chopped
Juice of 1 lemon
21 bream

Melt the margarine in a saucepan and add onion salt, garlic salt, pepper, Worcestershire sauce, vinegar, onion and lemon juice and mix well.

Arrange the fish in a greased pan or grill basket. Broil for 12 to 15 minutes, basting every 5 minutes with the margarine mixture and turning twice.

Makes 8 to 10 servings.

Smoked Carp

1 large carp, dressed
1 (26-ounce) package salt

Sprinkle the fish inside and out with salt. Place in a glass dish or bowl and let stand for 8 hours or refrigerate for 8 hours or more. Rinse thoroughly with cold water. Smoke over charcoal with wet hickory chips until golden brown.

Makes 6 to 8 servings.

Smoking a Fish

Season a whole cleaned fish with lemon juice, salt and pepper to taste. Let stand in a glass dish for 30 minutes. Place the fish on a rack in a smoker over charcoal and wet hickory chips. Smoke for 2 hours. Serve whole, or remove and serve portions.

Carp Balls

1 (3-pound) carp
1/4 cup salt
2 quarts water
2 cups cooked diced potatoes
Dash pepper
2 eggs, beaten
2 tablespoons melted butter
3 tablespoons heavy cream
Vegetable oil for deep-frying

Soak the whole fish in a mixture of salt and 1 quart of the water in a large container for at least 8 hours. Drain. Combine the fish and the remaining 1 quart fresh water in a large pan. Bring to a boil. Boil for 25 minutes. Remove the bones and skin from the fish. Combine 1 1/2 cups flaked fish, diced potatoes, pepper, eggs, butter and cream in a large bowl and mix well. Roll the mixture into 1-inch balls and fry in hot oil in a skillet. Makes 4 to 6 servings.

Cheese-Topped Catfish

2 pounds catfish fillets, cut into 6 serving portions
1 (10-ounce) can cream of tomato soup
2 tablespoons chopped onion
3/4 teaspoon salt
Dash pepper
1 cup shredded Cheddar cheese

Arrange the fish in one layer in a greased baking dish. Combine the soup, onion, salt and pepper in a bowl and mix well. Pour over the fish. Sprinkle with the cheese. Bake at 350 degrees for 25 minutes or until the fish flakes easily when tested with a fork. Makes 6 servings.

Catfish Potato Cakes

1 pound catfish fillets
3 eggs, beaten
2 tablespoons flour
2 tablespoons grated onion
1 tablespoon parsley, chopped
2 tablespoons salt
Dash nutmeg
Dash pepper
2 cups grated fresh potatoes

Skin the fillets and chop finely. Combine the fish, eggs, flour, onion, parsley, salt, nutmeg, pepper and potatoes in a large bowl and mix well. Spoon 1/3-cup portions of the fish mixture onto a hot greased griddle or skillet. Flatten slightly with a spatula. Fry until browned on one side. Turn and brown the other side. Total cooking time will be 6 to 8 minutes per cake. Drain on paper towels and keep warm. Serve with applesauce and sauerkraut. Makes 12 cakes.

Catfish and Spaghetti Casserole

1 (4-ounce) can mushroom pieces
2 tablespoons vegetable oil
2 tablespoons flour
1 teaspoon salt
1/4 teaspoon pepper
1 1/4 cups milk
1 cup shredded Cheddar cheese
2 tablespoons chopped pimentos
2 cups flaked cooked catfish
2 cups cooked spaghetti
1 tablespoon vegetable oil
1/2 cup dry bread crumbs

Drain the mushrooms, reserving the liquid. Heat 2 tablespoons oil in a saucepan over medium-low heat. Add the flour, salt and pepper and mix well. Add the milk and mushroom liquid gradually, stirring until smooth. Cook until thickened, stirring constantly. Add the cheese, pimentos, mushrooms and fish and mix well. Spoon half the spaghetti into a greased baking dish. Top with half the fish mixture. Repeat the layers. Combine 1 tablespoon oil with the bread crumbs in a bowl. Sprinkle over the casserole. Bake at 350 degrees for 30 minutes or until top is browned. Makes 4 to 6 servings.

Catfish in Court Bouillon

- 2 cups chopped onions
- 3/4 cup chopped green bell pepper
- 3/4 cup chopped celery
- 2 tablespoons butter
- 4 garlic cloves, minced
- 1 1/2 lemons, sliced
- 2 tablespoons ketchup
- 1 (6-ounce) can tomato paste
- 1 1/2 cups Fish Stock (see below)
- Salt and cayenne pepper to taste
- 4 pounds catfish fillets, cut into chunks

Sauté the onions, bell pepper and celery in butter in a pot over medium-low heat until tender. Add the garlic, lemon slices, ketchup, tomato paste and Fish Stock and mix well. Simmer over low heat for 30 minutes. Add the salt, cayenne pepper and catfish. Simmer for 25 minutes longer without stirring. Makes 8 to 10 servings.

Fish Stock

- 1 gallon plus 2 cups water
- Shrimp shells
- 1 catfish carcass
- 2 catfish fillets, chopped
- Celery leaves and tops
- 1 onion, chopped
- 1 carrot, halved
- 8 peppercorns
- Dash salt

Combine the water, shrimp shells, catfish carcass, catfish fillets, celery, onion, carrot, peppercorns and salt in a soup pot. Bring to a boil. Reduce the heat and simmer for 30 to 45 minutes. Strain out and discard the solids. Makes about 1 gallon.

Robbie's Catfish Gumbo

- $1^1/2$ cups peanut oil
- $1^1/4$ cups flour
- 2 cups chopped onions
- 1 cup chopped celery
- 1/2 cup diced bell pepper
- 6 garlic cloves, crushed
- 1 gallon fish stock, heated
- 1 pound crab meat
- 2 pounds catfish fillets, cut into 1-inch cubes
- 1 pound peeled shrimp
- 1 cup sliced green onions
- Salt and cayenne pepper to taste

Heat a large cast-iron Dutch oven or soup pot until it smokes. Add the peanut oil and heat. Sift the flour into the hot oil. Reduce the heat. Cook until the mixture is chocolate brown, stirring constantly. Add the onions, celery, bell pepper and garlic and cook until tender. Add the stock and crab meat and mix well. Reduce the heat and simmer for 30 minutes. Add the catfish, shrimp and green onions and simmer for 15 minutes longer. Add the salt and cayenne pepper. Serve over hot cooked rice.
Makes 10 to 12 servings.

Catfish Chowder

- 3 pounds catfish fillets
- 2 quarts plus 2 cups cold water
- 1 pound salt pork, diced
- 3 medium onions, diced
- 1 tablespoon salt
- 1 tablespoon white pepper
- 2 carrots, finely chopped
- 1/4 cup (1/2 stick) margarine
- 3 medium potatoes, diced
- 2 tablespoons parsley, finely chopped
- 1/4 cup cornstarch
- 1 quart half-and-half

Combine the catfish and cold water to cover in a soup pot. Bring to a boil, reduce heat, cover and simmer for 25 minutes. Remove from liquid and flake fish with a fork. Reserve liquid in soup pot.

Fry the salt pork in a skillet over medium heat until transparent. Drain. Add the onions to the skillet and cook until tender.

Add the fish, salt pork mixture, salt, pepper, carrots, margarine, potatoes and parsley to fish cooking liquid. Bring to a simmer and simmer for 10 minutes. Combine the cornstarch and enough cold water in a cup to make a thin paste. Add the paste to the soup pot. Cook for 5 minutes or until the chowder thickens slightly, stirring constantly. Turn off the heat. Stir in the half-and-half.
Makes 18 servings.

Crappie Amandine

2 eggs
1 cup milk
2 pounds crappie fillets
1 cup flour
1 teaspoon Lawry's seasoned salt
Peanut oil for frying
1/4 cup (1/2 stick) margarine
1 teaspoon Worcestershire sauce
1 teaspoon lemon juice
1/2 cup sliced almonds

Combine the eggs and milk in a bowl and mix well. Dip the fish into the egg mixture. Coat with the flour combined with the seasoned salt. Fry in hot oil in a skillet until golden brown. Drain on paper towels. Melt the margarine in a saucepan. Add the Worcestershire sauce and lemon juice. Place the fish on a broiler pan. Drizzle with the margarine mixture. Sprinkle with the almonds. Broil for 1 to 2 minutes or until the nuts are toasted. Makes 4 servings.

Oven-Baked Crappie

10 (3- to 5-ounce) crappie fillets
1 cup milk
1 cup self-rising flour
1/4 teaspoon Lawry's seasoned salt
1/2 cup peanut oil
1/2 cup (1 stick) margarine
2 tablespoons lemon juice
1 tablespoon parsley, chopped
Lemon slices

Marinate the fish in the milk in a shallow pan for 20 minutes. Remove the fish. Coat with the flour combined with the seasoned salt. Heat the peanut oil and 4 tablespoons of the margarine in a skillet until hot. Add the fish and cook until browned on both sides, turning once. Place the fish in a baking dish. Bake at 350 degrees for 8 minutes.

Combine the remaining 4 tablespoons margarine and the lemon juice in a saucepan. Heat until the margarine melts. Spoon over the cooked fish. Sprinkle with the parsley and top with lemon slices. Makes 8 to 10 servings.

Fried Crappie Fillets

8 crappie fillets
1 cup sour cream
2 cups baking mix
Dash black pepper
Dash cayenne pepper
Dash salt
Dash garlic salt
1 cup peanut oil

Combine the fish and sour cream in a bowl and refrigerate for 1 hour. Combine the baking mix, black pepper, cayenne pepper, salt and garlic salt in a bowl and mix well. Coat the fish with the mixture. Fry in hot oil in a skillet until golden brown. Drain on paper towels. Makes 6 to 8 servings.

Tips for Frying Fish

Select an oil that can be heated to a high temperature without smoking. Vegetable oils are preferable to animals fats, and peanut oil and safflower oil are good choices. Olive oil is not, as it has a very low smoke point.

Fish may be dipped into a liquid and coated with cornmeal or flour, or they may be dipped into a batter. The coating will keep the fish moist during frying and give it a delicious crispness.

Heat the oil to 350 degrees. At this temperature, the crust cooks quickly and the juices are held in the food. In addition, 350-degree oil doesn't soak into the fish. Total frying time at this temperature should be 4 to 5 minutes.

When frying in a skillet, place one layer of fish at a time in the skillet or pot and allow enough room so that pieces do not touch each other.

Drain fried fish on paper towels.

When frying large quantities of fish try this: place paper towels in the bottom of large brown paper bags. Place the cooked fish in the bags and close the top. This method will keep the fish hot as the paper absorbs grease.

Gilley's Sac-a-Lait (Crappie)

4 (1-pound) sac-a-lait, cleaned
Dash salt
Dash cayenne pepper
1 lemon
2 tablespoons margarine

Season one side of each fish with salt and cayenne pepper. Place seasoned side down in a greased baking dish. Score the top of the fish. Cut the lemon into halves and squeeze about 1 tablespoon lemon juice over the scored side. Broil for 8 minutes. Juice the lemon and combine the remaining juice with 2 tablespoons margarine in a saucepan. Cook over low heat until the margarine melts. Spoon the sauce over the fish. Broil the fish for 6 to 8 minutes longer or until it flakes easily. Makes 4 servings.

Baked Crappie

3 large crappie, scaled and drawn
Lawry's seasoned salt to taste
1/4 cup Italian salad dressing
1/2 cup (1 stick) margarine, melted
1/3 cup lemon juice

Score the fish on the diagonal across each side. Rub with seasoned salt. Combine with the salad dressing in a glass baking dish. Let stand for 30 minutes. Bake the fish in the dressing at 375 degrees for 20 minutes. Combine the margarine and lemon juice in a bowl and mix well. Baste the fish with the mixture. Bake for 8 to 10 minutes longer or until golden brown. Makes 3 servings.

Smoked Crappie Ball

1 pound smoked crappie
1 tablespoon lemon juice
1 tablespoon Worcestershire sauce
8 ounces cream cheese
1/4 cup finely chopped onion
1/2 cup chopped pecans
1 tablespoon parsley flakes

Flake the fish with a fork. Combine the fish, lemon juice, Worcestershire sauce, cream cheese and onion in a bowl and mix well. Shape the mixture into a ball. Roll in the pecans, then parsley. Serve as a spread for crackers. You may substitute smoked bass for crappie. Makes 32 servings.

Crappie Spread

Fillets of 2 crappie
1 teaspoon dillweed or seeds
1 teaspoon lemon juice
1/2 cup finely chopped white onion
1/4 cup chopped green bell pepper
1/4 cup chopped black olives
Salt and pepper to taste
1/2 cup mayonnaise

Combine the fish and water to cover in a saucepan. Add the dillweed and lemon juice to pan. Bring to a boil and boil for 3 to 5 minutes or until the fish is cooked through. Drain and cool the fish. Flake the fish with a fork. Combine with the onion, bell pepper, olives, salt, pepper and mayonnaise in a bowl and mix well. Serve with crackers. Makes about 28 servings.

Baked Redfish

1 cup (2 sticks) margarine
Dash each of salt and pepper
30 to 35 ounces prepared spaghetti sauce
1 (7-ounce) can mushrooms, drained
1 (5- to 8-pound) redfish

Melt the margarine in a skillet over medium heat. Add the salt, pepper, spaghetti sauce and mushrooms and mix well. Simmer for 3 minutes. Place the fish in a roasting pan with a lid or arrange on aluminum foil and place in a baking dish. Baste with the sauce and bake, covered or wrapped in the foil, at 400 degrees for 1 hour. Makes 6 to 8 servings.

How to Know the Fish You Buy Is Fresh

The flesh of fresh fish should have some bounce to it: when you press it, it should return to its natural shape. The eyes should be clear and bright. The skin should be shiny and the gills should be red. The odor should be clean and mild. If the tail of the fish is brittle, broken, or jagged, the fish probably has been frozen and defrosted.

"Contraband Crab Meat" (Gaspergou or Redfish)

2 quarts water
1 (4-ounce) package crab boil
1 teaspoon salt
1 teaspoon pepper
1 tablespoon lemon juice
1 large onion, quartered
4 medium gaspergou fillets, or 1 large redfish, filleted

Combine the water, crab boil, salt, pepper, lemon juice and onion in a large pot. Bring to a boil over medium-high heat. Add the fish. Boil until the fish flakes easily. Remove from the liquid and cool. Flake the fish and use it instead of crab meat for gumbo, as stuffing for baked fish or over a green salad. Makes $1^1/_2$ cups.

Note: A gaspergou is a freshwater drum.

Blackened Fish

6 (6- to 10-ounce) fish fillets
2 tablespoons blackening seasoning
1 cup (2 sticks) melted butter

This recipe should be prepared outside, as it creates an enormous amount of smoke and a dangerously hot cooking surface. On a gas burner or other portable cooking surface, heat a cast-iron Dutch oven to white hot. Sprinkle each fillet all over with seasoning. Dip the fish into the butter to coat completely. Drop into the hot Dutch oven and cook for 25 to 30 seconds on each side. Cook only 1 fillet at a time. Serve with hush puppies and coleslaw.
Makes 6 servings.

How Much Fish to Buy

For an average serving of $3^1/_2$ to 4 ounces of edible, cooked, boneless fish:

Buy one pound of whole fish per person;
Buy one-half pound of dressed fish or chunk of fish per person;
Buy 4 ounces of fillets, sticks, or steaks per person.

Fish in a Bag

3 cups water
1 teaspoon salt
1 bay leaf
2 lemon slices
Dash thyme
2 pounds fish fillets
2 tablespoons vegetable oil
2 tablespoons butter
1/2 cup sliced green onions
2 garlic cloves, minced
3 tablespoons flour
1/4 teaspoon salt
2 egg yolks, beaten
3 tablespoons dry white wine
1 (7-ounce) can crab meat, drained
1/4 pound cooked peeled shrimp

Combine the water, 1 teaspoon salt, bay leaf, lemon and thyme in a skillet and bring to a boil over medium-high heat. Add the fish. Reduce the heat, cover and simmer for 10 minutes or until the fish flakes easily with a fork. Remove the fish from liquid. Strain the liquid, discarding the solids and reserving the liquid. Handle the fillets gently to keep them intact.

Cut 6 pieces of brown paper or parchment into 10-by-12-inch hearts. Brush all over with oil. Place 1 fillet on one side of each heart. Set aside.

Melt the butter in a skillet. Add the green onions and garlic. Cook until tender, stirring occasionally. Add the flour and 1/4 teaspoon salt and mix well. Stir in the reserved liquid. Cook until thickened, stirring constantly. Stir a small amount of hot mixture into the egg yolks. Stir the egg yolks back into the sauce. Cook just until thick, stirring constantly. Remove from heat and stir in the wine, crab meat and shrimp. Spoon 1/2 cup sauce over each fillet. Fold the heart over each fillet to form individual packages. Seal by turning edges up and folding. Twist the tip of the heart to hold package closed. Place the packages in a baking pan. Bake at 400 degrees for 10 to 15 minutes. To serve, cut packages open with a large X on top. Fold back each segment. Makes 6 servings.

The Most Economical Forms of Fish to Buy

Whole fish is about 45 percent edible
Drawn fish is about 50 percent edible
Dressed fish is about 65 percent edible
Steaks and chunks are about 85 percent edible
Fillets are 100 percent edible

Grilled Barbecued Fish

- 1/2 cup lemon juice
- 1/4 cup white vinegar
- 1 teaspoon salt
- 1/2 teaspoon black pepper
- 1/2 teaspoon chopped garlic
- 1/2 teaspoon paprika
- 1/4 teaspoon cayenne pepper
- 1 1/2 teaspoons dry mustard
- 1/4 teaspoon Tabasco sauce
- 2 pounds fish fillets

Combine the lemon juice, vinegar, salt, black pepper, garlic, paprika, cayenne pepper, mustard and Tabasco sauce in a saucepan and mix well. Heat over medium heat until boiling. Grill the fish over hot coals for about 10 minutes per inch of thickness or until it flakes easily when tested with a fork, brushing often with warm barbecue sauce. Makes 4 to 6 servings.

Stuffed Fish

- 2 tablespoons margarine
- 1/4 cup chopped onion
- 1/4 cup chopped red bell pepper
- 1/4 cup chopped green bell pepper
- 10 (1/4-inch) slices dry French bread, cut into cubes
- 1 1/2 cups white bread cubes
- 1 (4-ounce) can shrimp, drained, chopped
- 1/4 cup clam juice
- 1 egg
- 1 teaspoon chopped fresh cilantro
- 1/4 teaspoon salt
- Dash cayenne pepper
- 4 (8-ounce) drawn fish
- 2 tablespoons margarine, melted
- Black pepper to taste
- 2 tablespoons white wine

Melt 2 tablespoons margarine in a skillet. Add the onion and bell peppers and cook for 3 minutes or until tender. Remove from heat. Combine with the bread cubes, shrimp, clam juice, egg, cilantro, salt and cayenne pepper in a large bowl and mix well. Brush the fish inside and out with 2 tablespoons margarine. Sprinkle evenly with black pepper. Arrange cavity up in a greased square baking dish. Prop the fish up with pieces of crushed aluminum foil. Divide the stuffing mixture among fish, stuffing into cavity. Drizzle with the wine mixed with any remaining margarine. Bake at 375 degrees for 15 to 20 minutes or until fish is firm, opaque and just barely flakes when tested with a fork. Makes 4 servings.

White Water Fish

$1\frac{1}{2}$ quarts (6 cups) water
2 onions, quartered
3 ribs celery
Salt and pepper to taste
1 teaspoon grated fresh gingerroot
3 to 4 pounds whole cleaned fish (bass or crappie work well)
Chopped green onions
2 tablespoons soy sauce
1 cup peanut oil

Combine the water, onions, celery, salt, pepper and gingerroot in a large pot. Bring to a boil. Add the fish. Boil for 8 to 10 minutes. Drain and discard the liquid and vegetables. Place the fish in a glass baking dish. Sprinkle with salt, pepper, green onions and soy sauce. Bring the peanut oil to a boil in a saucepan. Pour over the fish slowly. Serve hot. Makes 4 servings.

Fish au Gratin

2 tablespoons butter
2 tablespoons flour
$\frac{1}{2}$ teaspoon salt
2 cups milk
$\frac{3}{4}$ cup shredded Swiss cheese
1 tablespoon Worcestershire sauce
2 cups flaked cooked fish

Melt the butter in a saucepan over medium-low heat. Add the flour and salt and mix well. Add the milk gradually. Cook until the mixture bubbles and is thick, stirring constantly. Add the cheese and mix well. Cook until the cheese is melted. Stir in the Worcestershire sauce and fish and mix well. Fill greased individual ramekins. Bake at 350 degrees for 20 minutes or until browned on top. Makes 6 servings.

Fish and Cheese Bake

2 pounds fish fillets
Ranch salad dressing
1/2 pound mild Cheddar cheese, shredded
1 (7-ounce) package potato chips

Brush the fish with ranch salad dressing all over. Place in a baking dish. Sprinkle with the cheese. Crumble the potato chips and spread over the fish and cheese. Bake at 350 degrees for 15 minutes or until the fish flakes easily when tested with a fork. Makes 4 servings.

Fish Loaf

2 cups flaked cooked fish
1/2 cup cracker crumbs
1 cup milk
2 eggs, beaten
Salt and pepper to taste
1/2 cup canned cream of tomato soup
1/2 cup water

Combine the fish, cracker crumbs, milk, eggs, salt and pepper in a bowl and mix well. Form into a loaf in a greased loaf pan. Bake at 350 degrees for 10 minutes. Combine the soup and water and pour over the loaf. Bake for 20 minutes longer or until cooked through. Makes 4 to 6 servings.

Summer Fish and Potato Salad

1 cup flaked cooked fish
1 cup cooked diced potatoes
1 tablespoon diced green bell pepper
1/4 cup chopped celery
1 bacon slice, crisp-fried and crumbled
1/4 cup diced cucumber
1 tablespoon chopped onion
1 teaspoon salt
Pepper to taste
2 tablespoons mayonnaise

Combine the fish, potatoes, bell pepper, celery, bacon, cucumber and onion in a bowl and mix well. Season with the salt and pepper. Add the mayonnaise and mix well. Add more mayonnaise if needed to bind the ingredients together. Makes 4 servings.

Seviche

- 1 pound diced firm white fish fillets (crappie or bass work well)
- 2 bay leaves
- Salt and pepper to taste
- 1 cup lemon juice
- 1/2 teaspoon oregano
- 1/3 teaspoon garlic salt
- 1 white onion, diced
- 1 green bell pepper, diced
- 1 tomato, diced
- 3 jalapeño peppers, seeded, chopped
- 3 cups white vinegar
- 1 cup water
- 3 tablespoons chopped fresh parsley
- 2 tablespoons chopped fresh cilantro
- 1 tablespoon sugar

Combine the fish, bay leaves, salt, pepper, lemon juice, oregano and garlic salt in a glass or plastic bowl and mix well. Refrigerate, covered, for 8 to 10 hours.

Combine the onion, bell pepper, tomato, jalapeño peppers, vinegar and water in a bowl and mix well. Refrigerate, covered, for 2 to 3 hours. Drain the liquid from the fish and discard the bay leaves. Drain and discard the liquid from the vegetables. Combine the fish and vegetables in a bowl and mix well. Add the parsley, cilantro and sugar and mix well. Add more salt if needed. Serve with crackers. Makes 4 servings.

Fish Hash

- 2 cups cooked flaked fish
- 2 cups cooked diced potatoes
- 1 tablespoon minced onion
- 1 egg, beaten
- 1/2 teaspoon salt
- 1/4 teaspoon pepper
- 1 cup vegetable oil

Combine the fish, potatoes, onion, egg, salt and pepper in a bowl and mix well. Pour into hot oil in a skillet. Fry until golden brown, turning once. Fold omelet-style and serve. Makes 6 servings.

Fish Gumbo

- 1 pound whole fish
- 1/2 cup chopped celery
- 1/2 cup chopped green bell pepper
- 1/2 cup chopped onion
- 1 garlic clove, finely chopped
- 1/4 cup vegetable oil
- 2 beef bouillon cubes
- 2 cups boiling water
- 1 (10-ounce) can diced tomatoes and green chiles
- 1 (10-ounce) package frozen cut okra
- 1/4 teaspoon pepper
- 1/2 tablespoon salt
- 1/4 teaspoon thyme
- 1 bay leaf
- Dash Tabasco sauce

Combine the fish and water to cover in a pan. Bring to a boil over medium-high heat. Boil until the fish is cooked through. Skin and debone the fish.

Cook the celery, bell pepper, onion and garlic in oil in a soup pot over medium heat until tender. Add the bouillon cubes, boiling water, tomatoes, okra, pepper, salt, thyme, bay leaf and Tabasco sauce and mix well. Simmer, covered, for 30 minutes. Add the fish. Simmer, covered, for 20 minutes longer. Do not allow mixture to boil. Remove bay leaf before serving. Serve over hot cooked rice. Makes 4 to 6 servings.

Fried Eel

- 2 pounds eel, cut into 1 1/2-inch lengths
- 1 cup flour
- 1 tablespoon Lawry's seasoned salt
- Salt and pepper to taste
- Peanut oil for frying

Coat the eel with flour combined with seasoned salt, salt and pepper. Fry in 375-degree oil in a skillet until golden brown. Serve hot. Makes 4 to 6 servings.

Fried Alligator

2 pounds alligator
2 cups milk
2 cups self-rising flour
1 tablespoon Lawry's seasoned salt
Peanut oil for deep-frying

Remove all of the fat from the alligator. Cut the meat into 1/2-inch cubes.

Combine the alligator and milk in a bowl and let stand for 45 minutes. Remove from the milk and coat with flour combined with seasoned salt. Fry in hot oil in a skillet until golden brown. Drain on paper towels. Serve hot. Makes 6 servings.

Alligator Stew

4 cups alligator meat, cut into small serving pieces
1/2 cup self-rising flour
Salt and pepper to taste
1/2 cup vegetable oil
1 (10-ounce) can diced tomatoes with green chiles
1 cup water
1/2 cup sliced green onion tops
1/2 cup chopped celery
3/4 cup finely chopped onion
1/2 cup finely chopped green bell pepper
1 tablespoon parsley flakes

Coat the alligator with flour combined with salt and pepper. Brown in hot oil in a Dutch oven. Add the tomatoes, water, green onions, celery, onion, bell pepper and parsley and mix well. Cook, covered, over medium heat for about 30 minutes. Add more water if needed. Serve over hot cooked rice. Makes 8 to 10 servings.

Boiled Crawfish

- 25 pounds live crawfish
- 1 (26-ounce) package salt
- 3 gallons water
- 3 tablespoons cayenne pepper
- 4 onions, quartered
- 2 tablespoons prepared mustard
- 6 lemons, cut into wedges
- 2 cups salt
- 3 bags crab boil
- 1 (12-ounce) can beer
- Salt to taste

Combine the crawfish, water to cover and 1 package salt in a large soup pot or other large container. Let stand for 15 minutes to purge crawfish. Bring 3 gallons of water, cayenne pepper, onions, mustard, lemons and 2 cups salt to a boil in a lobster pot or other very large pot. Add the crab boil and boil for 8 minutes. Add the crawfish. Return to a boil. Boil for 7 minutes, adding the beer during the last minute of cooking time. Turn off the heat. Cover the lobster pot. Let stand for 5 minutes. Drain or strain out the crawfish. Salt generously. Makes 10 servings.

Crawfish Étouffée

- 1/2 cup (1 stick) butter
- 1 green bell pepper, chopped
- 5 ribs celery, chopped
- 1 bunch green onions, sliced
- 3 garlic cloves, chopped
- 1 pound crawfish meat
- 4 ounces crawfish fat (optional)
- Salt and red pepper to taste
- 2 tablespoons chopped parsley

Melt the butter in a large skillet over low heat and add the bell pepper, celery, green onions and garlic. Cook for 1 hour, stirring occasionally. Add the crawfish meat, fat, salt, red pepper and parsley and cook for 20 minutes longer. Serve with hot cooked rice. Makes 4 to 6 servings.

Quick Creamed Crawfish

1 cup (2 sticks) butter
2 yellow onions, chopped
1 green bell pepper, chopped
2 ribs celery, chopped
2 (10-ounce) cans cream of mushroom soup
1 (10-ounce) can cream of shrimp soup
1 pound crawfish meat

Melt the butter in a large skillet over medium-high heat and sauté the onions, bell pepper and celery until tender. Add the soups and mix well. Simmer over low heat for 30 minutes. Add the crawfish and cook for 30 minutes longer. You may use shrimp instead of crawfish. Makes 4 to 6 servings.

Fried Crawfish

2 pounds crawfish meat
Salt and pepper to taste
2 eggs
2 cups milk
1½ cups self-rising flour
Peanut oil for frying

Season the crawfish with salt and pepper. Combine the eggs and milk in a bowl and mix well. Dip the crawfish into the egg mixture, then coat with flour. Fry in hot oil in a skillet until golden brown. Makes 6 to 8 servings.

Frogs' Legs with Wine

18 pairs frogs' legs
2 cups flour
Salt and pepper to taste
Vegetable oil for frying
2 tablespoons butter
1 (4-ounce) can mushrooms, drained
½ cup chopped onion
¼ cup chopped parsley
½ cup dry white wine

Coat the frogs' legs in the flour combined with salt and pepper. Fry in hot oil in a skillet until golden brown. Melt the butter in another skillet. Add the mushrooms, onion and parsley and sauté until tender. Add salt and pepper. Place the frogs' legs on a warmed platter. Cover with the mushroom mixture. Pour the wine over the top. Makes 6 servings.

Baked Frogs' Legs

- 8 pairs frogs' legs
- 1/2 bottle dry white wine
- Garlic salt and lemon pepper to taste
- Dash lemon juice
- 1/2 cup (1 stick) butter
- 1/2 cup olive oil
- 2 to 4 garlic cloves
- Pimento strips for garnish
- Chopped parsley for garnish
- 1 (4-ounce) jar sliced mushrooms, drained, for garnish

Arrange the frogs' legs in a single layer in a large skillet. Add the wine, garlic salt, lemon pepper and lemon juice to the skillet. Bring to a boil, covered, over medium heat. Reduce the heat to medium-low and simmer for 5 minutes. Remove the frogs' legs. Arrange in an ovenproof serving dish. Discard the liquid in the skillet. Melt the butter with the olive oil in skillet over medium heat Add the garlic and sauté for 1 minute. Pour over the frogs' legs. Garnish with the pimento, parsley and mushrooms. Bake at 350 degrees for about 15 minutes or until hot. Makes 4 servings.

Country-Fried Frogs' Legs

- 10 pairs frogs' legs
- 2 cups milk
- 2 cups flour
- 1/2 teaspoon cayenne pepper
- Dash salt
- 3 eggs, beaten
- 1 cup bread crumbs
- 3 cups peanut oil
- 1 tablespoon margarine

Combine the frogs' legs and milk in a bowl and let stand for 30 to 45 minutes. Remove from the milk. Coat with the flour combined with cayenne pepper and salt. Dip into the beaten eggs. Coat with the bread crumbs. Fry in 350-degree oil and margarine in a large skillet until golden brown. Makes 4 servings.

Breaded Frogs' Legs

6 pairs frogs' legs
Salt and pepper to taste
3 tablespoons lemon juice
2 eggs, beaten
1 cup fine bread crumbs
3 cups vegetable oil

Season the frogs' legs with salt, pepper and lemon juice. Dip into the eggs. Coat with the bread crumbs. Fry in hot oil in a large skillet for 3 to 4 minutes or until golden brown. Makes 2 or 3 servings.

Turtle Steak and Gravy

2 pounds turtle meat
Salt, pepper and garlic salt to taste
Flour
1 cup vegetable oil
3 tablespoons butter
1 garlic clove, chopped
1 (10-ounce) can cream of mushroom soup
1/3 cup red wine
1/3 cup capers
1/3 cup milk

Cut the steaks cross grain. Pound with a meat mallet. Season with salt, pepper and garlic salt. Coat with flour. Work the flour into the meat with a fork. Fry in hot oil in a large skillet until browned. Remove from the skillet. Drain the oil from the skillet. Add the butter and garlic to the skillet. Simmer over low heat for 10 minutes. Add the soup, wine and capers and mix well. Add milk and mix well. Place meat in gravy. Cook for 10 minutes.
Makes 4 to 6 servings.

Turtle Stew

2 pounds turtle meat
2 quarts water
1/2 pound salt pork
1/4 cup (1/2 stick) butter
1 garlic clove
1 large onion, chopped
Flour
1 (10-ounce) can cream of tomato soup
1 cup diced potato

Cut the turtle meat into bite-size pieces. Boil in 2 quarts water in a large pot for 20 minutes. Drain and reserve the liquid. Fry the salt pork in a Dutch oven over medium heat. Drain all but 2 tablespoons of oil. Add the butter and garlic. Reduce heat and cook until lightly browned. Add the onion. Coat the turtle with flour and add to the Dutch oven. Cook until turtle is lightly browned. Pour part of the reserved cooking liquid into the Dutch oven and mix well. Simmer, covered, for several hours or until turtle is tender. Add the tomato soup, potato and remaining stock. Cook for 30 minutes longer. Makes 8 servings.

Turtle Soup

1 pound turtle meat
1 quart plus 2 cups water
1 (10-ounce) can cream of tomato soup
1 large onion, chopped
1 rib celery, chopped
1 green bell pepper, chopped
1 teaspoon salt
1/2 cup barley
1/2 cup red wine
2 tablespoons lemon juice
2 tablespoons Worcestershire sauce

Combine the turtle, water, soup, onion, celery, bell pepper and salt in a soup pot and place over low heat. Simmer for 1 hour. Stir in the barley and cook for 30 minutes longer. Stir in the wine, lemon juice and Worcestershire sauce. Simmer for 10 minutes longer. Serve hot. Makes 4 servings.

Simmered Turtle in Wine

- 2 pounds turtle meat
- Flour
- Salt and pepper to taste
- 1 cup vegetable oil
- 1 tablespoon minced onion
- 3/4 cup red wine
- 3/4 cup water

Cut the turtle meat into chunks. Coat with flour combined with salt and pepper. Brown in hot oil in a skillet. Reduce heat to low, add the onion, wine and water and mix well. Simmer, covered, until the turtle is tender. Makes 4 to 6 servings.

Fried Turtle

- 1 medium turtle, cut into serving pieces
- 1 teaspoon salt
- 1/2 teaspoon pepper
- 2 bay leaves
- Flour
- Salt and pepper to taste
- Butter
- Milk

Combine the turtle, water to cover, 1 teaspoon salt, pepper and bay leaves in a pot. Bring to a boil and boil for 15 minutes. Drain. Dust the turtle with flour combined with salt and pepper. Fry in butter in a large skillet until tender and golden brown. To make gravy from the pan drippings, estimate the number of tablespoons of drippings and stir in 1 tablespoon of flour per tablespoon drippings. Cook over low heat until well blended, stirring constantly. Add 1 cup of milk per tablespoon of flour and cook until thickened, stirring constantly. Makes 4 servings.

Cajun Fettuccini

3 medium onions, chopped
3 bell peppers, chopped
2 jalapeño peppers, seeded and chopped
1/4 bunch parsley, chopped
1 1/2 cups (3 sticks) butter
1/4 cup flour
Dash cayenne pepper
2 tablespoons lemon juice
1 pound Velveeta cheese, cubed
3 pounds shrimp or crawfish, peeled
1 pound crab meat
1 cup half-and-half
1 pound fettuccini, cooked

Sauté the onions, bell peppers, jalapeño peppers and parsley in butter in a large skillet over medium heat until tender. Add the flour and cayenne pepper to the skillet and mix well. Cook until thickened, stirring constantly. Add the lemon juice, cheese, shrimp, crab meat and half-and-half and mix well. Cook until the cheese is melted and shrimp are opaque. Serve over pasta. Makes 12 servings.

Seafood Casserole

1 onion, chopped
1 green bell pepper, chopped
1/4 cup (1/2 stick) margarine
1 (10-ounce) can Cheddar cheese soup
1 (10-ounce) can cream of mushroom soup
1 pound fresh shrimp, shelled
1 pound crab meat
1 cup uncooked rice
Salt and pepper to taste
1/2 cup bread crumbs

Saute the onion and bell pepper in margarine in a medium skillet over medium-high heat until tender. Combine with the soups, shrimp, crab meat, rice, salt and pepper in a large bowl and and mix well. Spoon into a greased baking dish. Sprinkle with the bread crumbs. Bake at 350 degrees for 1 1/4 hours. Makes 6 to 8 servings.

Cross Seafood Chowder

2 medium onions, chopped
1 rib celery, chopped
1/2 green bell pepper, chopped
1/2 cup (1 stick) butter
8 ounces cream cheese, cut into small pieces
2 (10-ounce) cans cream of potato soup
2 (10-ounce) cans baby clams
2 (4-ounce) cans small shrimp
2 (6-ounce) cans white crab meat
3 (5-ounce) catfish fillets, chopped (optional)
1 quart plus 1 pint (6 cups) half-and-half
10 ounces water
1/2 carrot, finely chopped
Dash white pepper
Dash salt (optional)

Sauté the onions, celery and bell pepper in butter in a large skillet over medium-high heat. Add the cream cheese, soup, clams, shrimp, crab meat, fish, half-and-half, water and carrot and mix well. Simmer over low heat for 30 minutes. Do not allow to boil. Add the pepper and salt. Serve hot. Makes 15 servings.

Oyster Fritters

1 cup pancake mix
1 teaspoon baking powder
Salt and pepper to taste
1 egg
2 tablespoons chopped onion
1 pint oysters, chopped
1/4 cup vegetable oil

Combine the pancake mix, baking powder, salt and pepper in a bowl and mix well. Add egg, onion and undrained oysters and mix well. Drop by tablespoonfuls into hot oil in a large skillet. Fry until browned all over. Drain on paper towels. Makes 30 fritters.

Ma Smith's Oyster Stew

2 tablespoons margarine
12 ounces oysters
1 tablespoon grated onion
3/4 cup finely crushed cracker crumbs
2 cups milk
Dash pepper or freshly ground pepper

Melt the margarine in a small soup pot over medium heat. Add the undrained oysters and onion. Simmer until the oysters curl. Remove from the heat. Add the cracker crumbs and stir until all the liquid in the soup pot is absorbed. Place the soup pot over low heat. Add the milk gradually, stirring with a slotted spoon. Cook until the mixture is the consistency of a medium white sauce. Add the pepper and heat mixture until hot. Do not boil. Makes 3 or 4 servings.

Robbie's Crab Meat Bake

1 rib celery, chopped
1/4 cup chopped onion
1/2 cup (1 stick) margarine
1/2 cup flour
2 cups heavy cream
2 egg yolks
1 tablespoon salt
1 1/2 teaspoons red pepper
1 teaspoon (scant) white pepper
1 pound lump crab meat
1/2 cup shredded mild Cheddar cheese
1/4 cup sliced green onions

Sauté the celery and onion in margarine in a medium skillet over medium heat until tender. Add the flour and mix well. Add the cream gradually, stirring constantly. Cook until thickened. Add the egg yolks, salt, red and white pepper. Pour the sauce over the crab meat in a large bowl and mix well. Spoon into a greased baking dish. Sprinkle with the cheese. Bake at 375 degrees for 10 to 15 minutes or until light brown. Sprinkle with the green onions. Makes 6 to 8 servings.

Boiled Crabs

24 live crabs
3 (26-ounce) packages salt
4 gallons water
2 (3-ounce) boxes crab boil
6 garlic cloves
2 tablespoons cayenne pepper
6 onions, quartered
6 lemons, quartered
Salt to taste

Combine the crabs, water to cover and 3 packages salt in a large container. Let stand for 20 minutes. Drain. Wash the crabs in fresh water. Combine 4 gallons water, crab boil, garlic, cayenne pepper and onions in a 6-gallon or other large pot. Squeeze the lemons into the pot and add the peels. Bring to a boil over high heat and boil, covered, for 12 minutes. Add the crabs and return to a boil. Cook, covered, for 10 minutes. Remove the crabs and salt liberally. Makes 6 servings.

Fried Soft-Shell Crabs

8 soft-shell crabs, cleaned
Dash salt
Dash pepper
2 eggs
1¼ cups milk
2 cups flour
4 cups vegetable oil

Season the crabs with salt and pepper. Combine the eggs and milk in a large bowl. Add the crabs and let stand for 20 to 30 minutes. Remove from mixture and coat with the flour. Fry in 350-degree oil in a deep skillet until golden brown. Serve hot with tartar sauce or cocktail sauce. Makes 2 servings.

Crab Cakes

1 pound lump crab meat
2 eggs, beaten
2 tablespoons mayonnaise
½ cup bread or cracker crumbs
Dash salt
Dash pepper
1 teaspoon dry mustard
2 teaspoons finely chopped parsley
1 teaspoon Worcestershire sauce
1 cup flour
2 cups vegetable oil

Combine the crab meat, eggs, mayonnaise, crumbs, salt, pepper, mustard, parsley and Worcestershire sauce in a large bowl and mix well. Shape into small cakes. Coat the cakes with flour. Fry in 350-degree oil in a skillet until golden brown. Serve hot. Makes 4 servings.

Outdoor Shrimp Boil

- 2 gallons water
- 1/2 bunch celery, chopped
- 2 (3-ounce) boxes crab boil
- 2 cups salt
- 2 1/2 pounds smoked sausage, cut into chunks
- 10 ears corn
- 5 pounds medium shrimp

Bring the water to a boil in a 3- to 5-gallon pot. Add the celery, crab boil and salt. Return to a boil. Add the sausage and boil for 6 minutes. Add the corn and boil for 5 minutes. Add the shrimp and boil for 5 minutes. To serve, drain or strain out the shrimp, sausage and corn and place on newspaper-covered table or in a tub. Makes 10 servings.

Shrimp Salad

- 4 cups peeled boiled shrimp
- 1/3 cup diced green bell pepper
- 1/2 cup sweet pickle relish
- 1/4 cup chopped celery
- 1/4 cup diced onion
- 1/2 cup sliced black olives
- 1/4 cup mayonnaise
- 3 tablespoons ketchup
- 1 1/2 tablespoons olive oil
- Salt and cayenne pepper to taste
- 4 hard-cooked eggs, quartered
- 4 large tomatoes, quartered
- 1/2 head iceberg lettuce, separated into leaves

Chop the shrimp into medium pieces. Combine the bell pepper, relish, celery, onion and olives in a large bowl and mix well. Add the mayonnaise, ketchup, olive oil, salt and cayenne pepper and mix gently. Arrange the salad, eggs and tomatoes on a lettuce leaf for each serving. Makes 4 to 6 servings.

Serve-Alongs

Serve-Alongs
Serve-Alongs
Serve-Alongs
Serve-Alongs
Serve-Alongs
Serve-Alongs
Serve-Alongs
Serve-Alongs

Beefy Bloody Mary Mix

1 (46-ounce) can tomato juice
1 (10-ounce) can beef consommé
1 teaspoon salt
1 tablespoon celery salt
3 tablespoons Tabasco sauce
1 (5-ounce) bottle Worcestershire sauce
1 tablespoon pepper
1/4 cup sugar
Juice of 3 lemons
2 tablespoons prepared horseradish
Vodka to taste

Combine the tomato juice, beef consommé, salt, celery salt, Tabasco sauce, Worcestershire sauce, pepper, sugar, lemon juice and horseradish in a large container and mix well. Refrigerate until serving. Stir before mixing with vodka to taste. Makes 10 servings.

Water Chestnut Dip

1 cup mayonnaise
1 (8-ounce) can water chestnuts, drained, finely chopped
2 teaspoons beef bouillon granules
1/4 teaspoon garlic powder
8 ounces sour cream
2 tablespoons chopped pimentos
3 tablespoons sliced green onions
1/2 teaspoon Worcestershire sauce

Combine the mayonnaise, water chestnuts, bouillon, garlic powder, sour cream, pimentos, green onions and Worcestershire sauce in a large bowl and mix well. Chill, covered, until serving time. Serve with crackers or toast. Makes about 40 servings.

Spinach Cheese Spread

2 (10-ounce) packages frozen chopped spinach
Salt and black pepper to taste
1 large onion, finely chopped
8 ounces fresh mushrooms
1 tablespoon margarine
8 ounces Cheddar cheese
8 ounces mozzarella cheese
8 ounces Colby cheese
4 ounces cream cheese
Dash Worcestershire sauce
2 loaves French bread
Dash cayenne pepper
Dash paprika

Cook the spinach according to package directions. Drain well. Season with salt and black pepper. Sauté the onion and mushrooms in margarine in a large skillet. Melt the Cheddar, mozzarella, Colby and cream cheese in the top of a double boiler over simmering water, stirring until well blended. Combine with the spinach, onion and mushrooms in a bowl and mix well. Season with the salt, black pepper and Worcestershire sauce.

Slice the bread. Spread the spinach mixture on each slice. Sprinkle lightly with cayenne pepper and paprika. Arrange on foil-covered baking sheet. Cover with aluminum foil. Bake at 350 degrees for 10 minutes. Makes 12 servings.

Shrimp Dip

1/2 pound shrimp, boiled, peeled, chopped
3/4 cup sour cream
3 green onions, sliced
3/4 cup mayonnaise
Salt to taste

Combine the shrimp, sour cream, green onions, mayonnaise and salt in a medium bowl and mix well. Chill, covered, until serving time. Serve with bite-size vegetables, chips or crackers. Makes about 40 servings.

Shrimp Spread

16 ounces cream cheese, softened
3 tablespoons minced onion
3 tablespoons Worcestershire sauce
2 teaspoons lemon juice
Dash Tabasco sauce
Dash pepper
2 (4-ounce) cans shrimp, drained, chopped

Beat the cream cheese with an electric mixer until fluffy. Add the onion, Worcestershire sauce, lemon juice, Tabasco sauce and pepper and mix well. Add the shrimp and mix well. Chill, covered, until serving time. Serve with crackers. Makes about 40 servings.

Marinated Vegetable Hors D'oeuvre

2 (4-ounce) cans mushroom stems and pieces, drained, chopped
1 (4-ounce) jar chopped pimentos, drained
1 (14-ounce) can artichoke hearts, drained, chopped
1/4 cup chopped bell pepper
1/4 cup chopped onion
1/2 cup chopped celery
2/3 cup white vinegar
1/4 cup sliced green onions with tops
1 teaspoon garlic salt
1 teaspoon sugar
1/2 teaspoon lemon pepper
2 1/2 teaspoons Italian seasoning
1 teaspoon Lawry's seasoned salt
1 teaspoon onion salt
2/3 cup olive oil

Combine the mushrooms, pimentos, artichoke hearts, bell pepper, onion and celery in a large bowl and mix well. Combine the vinegar, green onions, garlic salt, sugar, lemon pepper, Italian seasoning, seasoned salt, onion salt and olive oil in a medium saucepan. Bring to a boil over low heat. Boil for 5 minutes. Let stand until cool. Pour over the vegetables. Chill, covered, until ready to serve.
Makes 1 quart.

Chowchow

1 gallon fresh firm ripe tomatoes
1 quart chopped onions
1 pint chopped hot peppers
3 1/2 cups sugar
1 1/2 cups white vinegar
2 tablespoons salt

Cook the tomatoes in boiling water in a large pot for a few seconds then remove from the boiling water and place under cold running water. Peel the tomatoes and chop. Combine with the onions, peppers, sugar, vinegar and salt in a large pot. Cook over medium-low heat for 1 hour, stirring frequently. Mixture should be thick. Spoon into hot sterile canning jars. Top with sterile lids and rings. Process in a water bath for 10 minutes, making sure the water is at least 1 inch above tops of lids. Makes 12 pints.

Pickled Okra

3 1/2 pounds small okra, washed
5 small fresh hot peppers
5 garlic cloves, peeled
2 cups white vinegar
2 tablespoons dillseeds
1 cup water
2 tablespoons pickling salt

Cut off the okra stems. Pack the okra large end down into 5 sterile canning jars. Place 1 hot pepper and 1 garlic clove in each jar. Combine the vinegar, dillseeds, water and pickling salt in a saucepan and bring to a boil over medium-high heat. Pour over okra, leaving 1/4 inch of room at the top. Top with sterile lids and rings. Process for 10 minutes in a water bath, making sure the water is 1 inch above tops of lids. Makes 5 pints.

Hot Pepper Jelly

1 large green bell pepper, chopped
4 jalapeño peppers, chopped
2 cups water
1 cup white vinegar
5 cups sugar
3 drops red or green food coloring
1/3 cup fresh lemon juice
1 (6-ounce) bottle pectin

Combine the bell pepper, jalapeño peppers and water in a saucepan. Bring to a boil over medium heat and simmer, covered, until tender. Strain through a colander and then through cheesecloth. Combine the liquid with the vinegar, sugar and food coloring in a large saucepan. Bring to a boil. Add the lemon juice and pectin. Boil for 1 minute. Remove from the heat and skim the foam. Pour into hot sterile jars, leaving 1/4 inch of room at the top. Seal with sterile lids and rings. Turn upside down immediately. Let stand for 5 minutes, then turn right side up. Makes 4 pints.

Black Bean Soup

1 cup dried black beans
2 onions, chopped
6 garlic cloves, chopped
2 tablespoons margarine
1 pound link sausage, diced
2 (15-ounce) cans black beans with jalapeño peppers
4 chicken bouillon cubes
1 bay leaf
2 cups water
1/2 cup medium salsa

Soak the beans in water to cover in a pot for 8 to 10 hours. Drain. Sauté the onions and garlic in margarine in a medium skillet. Add the sausage and cook until browned. Drain the excess oil. Combine with the soaked beans, canned beans, bouillon cubes, bay leaf, water and salsa in a pot. Simmer for 1 hour or until the beans are tender. Remove the bay leaf. Serve the soup topped with sour cream and green onions. Makes 6 to 8 servings.

Cream of Any Vegetable Soup

$1^1/2$ pounds chopped yellow squash, carrots, green beans, broccoli, cauliflower, mushrooms, potatoes, tomatoes or a combination
1 onion, chopped
3 quarts chicken broth, or water with 12 chicken bouillon cubes
1/2 cup (1 stick) margarine
1 (5-ounce) can evaporated milk
3 pints half-and-half
Salt and pepper to taste

Combine the vegetables, onion and chicken broth in a soup pot. Cook over medium heat until the vegetables are tender. Purée the mixture in batches in a blender. Pour the purée through a strainer back into the soup pot. Add the margarine, evaporated milk, half-and-half, salt and pepper. Cook until heated through but do not boil. This freezes well. Makes 1 gallon.

Chitterlings

2 gallons water
2 tablespoons Lawry's seasoned salt
3 tablespoons cayenne pepper
1/3 cup salt
3 tablespoons garlic salt
2 large onions, chopped
3 gallons cleaned chitterlings
4 cups flour
Salt and black pepper to taste
2 cups peanut oil

Bring the water to a boil in a 5-gallon pot. Add the seasoned salt, cayenne pepper, salt, garlic salt and onions. Return to a boil. Add the chitterlings. Reduce the heat and boil gently for 2 hours. Remove and serve the chitterlings boiled. Or, to fry chitterlings, cut into 4- to 6-inch lengths for frying. Roll in flour seasoned with salt and black pepper. Fry in hot peanut oil in a skillet.
Makes 8 to 10 servings.

Dirty Rice

1 cup vegetable oil
1 cup flour
1 cup chopped onion
1 cup chopped celery
1 1/2 pounds chicken giblets
Salt, black pepper and red pepper to taste
1 quart water
2 garlic cloves, minced
2 1/2 cups cooked rice
1/2 cup sliced green onions
1/3 cup parsley

Heat the oil in a large saucepan over high heat. Add the flour and mix well. Reduce the heat and cook until the roux is golden brown, stirring constantly. Add the onion and celery and mix well. Cook until tender. Remove from heat and set aside. Season the giblets with salt, black pepper and red pepper. Simmer in the water with the garlic in a saucepan over medium-low heat until the giblets are tender. Strain out the giblets, reserving stock. Grind the giblets. Add the giblets and reserved stock to the roux. Cook until the mixture is the consistency of thick gravy, stirring constantly. Add the rice, green onions and parsley and cook until heated through. Makes 4 to 6 servings.

Red Beans and Rice

1 pound dried red kidney beans
1 meaty ham bone
1/2 cup parsley, chopped
3 large garlic cloves, crushed
1 bay leaf
1/2 teaspoon sugar
Dash Tabasco sauce
1/4 teaspoon thyme
1/4 teaspoon oregano
3 large onions, chopped
1 bunch green onions, chopped
1 tablespoon salt
Dash red pepper
1 teaspoon black pepper
1/2 cup ketchup
1 tablespoon Worcestershire sauce
1 1/2 pounds sausage
Hot cooked rice

Soak the beans in water to cover in a soup pot for 8 to 10 hours. Drain. Cover with fresh water. Add the ham bone to the pot. Cook over low heat for 3 hours or until beans are tender. Add the parsley, garlic, bay leaf, sugar, Tabasco sauce, thyme, oregano, onions, green onions, salt, red pepper, black pepper, ketchup and Worcestershire sauce. Simmer for 1 1/2 hours. Cut the sausage into bite-size pieces. Fry in a skillet over medium heat until cooked through; drain. Add to the soup pot and mix well. Remove the bay leaf. Serve the bean mixture over hot cooked rice.
Makes 10 servings.

Fruited Ginger Rice

1 cup rice
1/4 cup (1/2 stick) butter
1 (15-ounce) can fruit cocktail, drained
1/2 teaspoon ground ginger
1/4 cup sliced green onions

Cook the rice according to the package directions. Melt the butter in a medium saucepan. Add the fruit cocktail, ginger and green onions to the saucepan and mix well. Cook until heated through. Add to the cooked rice and mix well. Serve hot with baked quail, dove or other game birds. Makes 4 to 6 servings.

Baked Wild Rice Pilaf

1 1/2 cups wild rice
4 (10-ounce) cans beef consommé
3/4 cup chopped green bell pepper
1 cup chopped onion
1 cup mushrooms, sliced
1/4 cup (1/2 stick) margarine
Dash salt
Dash pepper
1 cup heavy cream

Cook the rice in the consommé in a saucepan over medium-low heat until all the liquid is absorbed. Sauté the bell pepper, onion and mushrooms in margarine in a skillet until tender. Add to the rice and mix well. Add the salt, pepper and cream and mix well. Spoon into a baking dish. Bake, uncovered, at 350 degrees for 25 minutes. Makes 4 to 6 servings.

Fluffy Rice

1 cup rice
1 tablespoon peanut oil or butter
2 cups water
1 teaspoon salt
1/2 teaspoon white vinegar

Combine the rice and water to cover in a bowl or pot. Stir to rinse rice. Drain. Combine the rice, peanut oil, 2 cups water, salt and vinegar in a large saucepan. Bring to a boil over medium-high heat. Reduce heat to medium-low. Cook until the rice and water are at the same level. Reduce heat to low. Cook, covered, for 15 to 20 minutes. Remove from heat and let stand for 10 minutes. Makes 4 servings.

Baked Cheese Grits

1 cup grits
1/2 cup (1 stick) butter
1 (8-ounce) package garlic cheese
1 (8-ounce) package jalapeño cheese
2 eggs, beaten
Milk
Salt to taste

Cook the grits in a saucepan according to package directions. Add the butter and cheeses to hot grits in the saucepan or a bowl. Mix well. Place the eggs in a measuring cup and add enough milk to measure 1 cup. Add to the grits mixture with salt and mix well. Pour into a baking dish. Bake at 350 degrees for 30 minutes or until top is brown. Makes 6 to 8 servings.

Corn Bread Dressing

- 1 large hen
- 3 quarts water
- 6 peppercorns
- 2 carrots, chopped
- 1 onion, chopped
- 2 ribs celery, chopped
- Salt to taste
- 6 onions, chopped
- 2 ribs celery, chopped
- 1/2 cup (1 stick) margarine
- 1/4 cup chicken-flavored soup base
- 1 teaspoon poultry seasoning
- 2 (8-inch) round pans 2-day-old Corn Bread for Dressing (below)
- 8 slices white bread, toasted and crumbled
- 2 eggs, beaten
- 6 hard-cooked eggs, chopped

Cut the hen into serving pieces. Combine with the water in a soup pot. Add the peppercorns, carrots, 1 onion, 2 ribs celery and salt. Bring to a boil over medium-high heat. Reduce heat to medium and boil for 1 hour or until the chicken is tender. Remove the chicken from the stock and let stand until cool enough to handle. Remove the skin and bones. Chop the meat. Strain the stock, discarding the solids. Skim the stock, discarding the fat. Sauté 6 onions and 2 ribs celery in 1/4 cup of the margarine in a large skillet or soup pot. Bring the stock to a boil in pot. Add the sautéed onions and celery, remaining margarine, chicken soup base and poultry seasoning and mix well.

Crumble the corn bread into a large bowl. Add the white bread and mix well. Add the chicken and mix well. Add the stock with onion and celery, stirring until mixture is of a soupy consistency. Add 2 beaten eggs and mix well. Add 6 hard-cooked eggs and salt to taste. Pour the mixture into 2 or 3 greased large rectangular baking dishes. Bake, covered, at 350 degrees for 45 minutes. Remove covers and bake for 45 minutes longer. Makes 20 to 24 servings.

Corn Bread for Dressing

- 6 cups self-rising cornmeal
- 2 cups self-rising flour
- 1 tablespoon baking powder
- 1 tablespoon sugar
- 2 eggs
- 3 cups milk
- 2 tablespoons vegetable oil

Combine the cornmeal, flour, baking powder and sugar in a bowl and mix well. Add eggs and milk and mix well. Grease three 10-inch pans with the oil. Heat in a 450-degree oven until hot. Pour excess oil into batter and mix well. Pour batter into hot pans. Bake until golden brown. Makes 3 pans.

Giblet Gravy for Dressing

- 2 cups uncooked dressing with chicken
- 2 cups chicken broth
- 2 hard-cooked eggs, chopped
- 1 tablespoon cornstarch
- 1 tablespoon chicken soup base

Combine the dressing, chicken broth, eggs, cornstarch and chicken soup base in a saucepan. Cook over low heat until thickened. Serve over dressing. Makes about 4 cups.

Jalapeño Corn Bread

- 3 cups corn bread mix
- 2 cups milk
- 1/2 cup vegetable oil
- 2 tablespoons sugar
- 1/2 cup jalapeño peppers, chopped
- 1 1/2 cups shredded sharp Cheddar cheese
- 1/4 pound bacon, crisp-fried, crumbled
- 1/4 cup pimentos, chopped
- 1 cup cream-style corn
- 2 large onions, finely chopped
- 2 eggs, beaten

Combine the corn bread mix and milk in a large bowl and mix well. Add the oil, sugar, jalapeño peppers, Cheddar cheese, bacon, pimentos, corn, onions, and eggs and mix well.

Grease two 10-inch cast-iron skillets or 25 cast-iron corn stick molds and place in a 450-degree oven until very hot. Pour in batter. Bake for 30 to 35 minutes or until light brown. Makes 12 servings.

Secret Ingredient Corn Bread

- $1^1/_2$ cups self-rising cornmeal
- $^1/_2$ cup self-rising flour
- 1 tablespoon sugar
- $1^1/_2$ cups milk
- 1 tablespoon mayonnaise
- 1 egg
- 1 tablespoon vegetable oil

Combine the cornmeal, flour and sugar in a large bowl and mix well. Combine the milk, mayonnaise and egg in a bowl and mix well. Add to cornmeal mixture and stir just until combined. Coat an 8-inch cast-iron skillet with the oil and heat in a 450-degree oven until hot. Pour the batter into the hot skillet and return to oven. Bake until top is brown. Makes 4 generous servings.

Cracklin' Bread

- 3 cups self-rising cornmeal
- 1 cup self-rising flour
- 1 tablespoon sugar
- 1 teaspoon baking powder
- 1 cup cracklings
- 1 tablespoon mayonnaise
- 1 egg
- 3 cups milk
- 2 tablespoons vegetable oil

Combine the cornmeal, flour, sugar and baking powder in a large bowl and mix well. Add the cracklings, mayonnaise, egg and milk and mix well. You may need additional milk to make of a batter consistency.

Grease a large rectangular baking pan with the oil and place in a 450-degree oven until hot. Pour or spoon batter into pan. Bake for about 25 to 30 minutes or until golden brown. Makes 6 to 8 servings.

For Perfectly Fluffy Corn Bread

Never pour batter into a cold skillet or corn bread will absorb all the grease and become soggy.

Cross Corn Bread

3 cups self-rising cornmeal
1 cup self-rising flour
2 tablespoons sugar
1 teaspoon baking powder
$1^1/2$ cups milk
1 egg
2 tablespoons peanut oil

Combine the cornmeal, flour, sugar, baking powder, milk and egg in a large bowl and mix well. Pour the peanut oil into a 10-inch cast-iron skillet. Heat in a 450-degree oven until hot. Pour the hot oil into the batter and mix well. Pour the batter into the skillet. Bake for 25 to 30 minutes or until golden brown. Makes 6 to 8 servings.

Cross Hush Puppies

1 egg
1 large green bell pepper, finely chopped
2 large onions, chopped
3 cups self-rising cornmeal
1 cup self-rising flour
1 tablespoon sugar
1 teaspoon baking powder
$1^1/2$ cups milk
4 cups vegetable oil

Combine the egg, bell pepper and onions in a large bowl and mix well. Add the cornmeal, flour, sugar and baking powder and mix well. Stir in the milk until the mixture is of a stiff consistency. Heat the oil to 350 degrees in a pot.

For perfectly round hush puppies, scoop out the batter with a size-10 melon scoop. Carefully drop the batter into the hot oil. Fry until golden brown. You may add a 4-ounce can of drained crab meat to the batter for crab fritters. Makes 75 hush puppies.

Beer Biscuits

3 cups baking mix
2 tablespoons sugar
9 ounces ($3/4$ can) beer

Combine the baking mix, sugar and beer in a bowl and mix well. Spoon into hot greased muffin cups. Bake at 350 degrees for about 10 minutes or until golden brown. Makes 18 biscuits.

Angel Biscuits

5 cups self-rising flour
1 teaspoon baking soda
$1/3$ cup sugar
1 cup shortening
2 envelopes yeast dissolved in $1/4$ cup warm water
2 cups buttermilk, at room temperature

Sift the flour, baking soda and sugar in a bowl. Cut in the shortening with a pastry cutter or 2 knives until the mixture resembles coarse crumbs. Add the dissolved yeast and buttermilk and mix well. Refrigerate, covered, for at least 2 hours and up to 10 hours. Pinch off dough with floured hands and shape into biscuits. Place the biscuits on a greased baking sheet. Let rise for 1 to 2 hours. Bake at 425 degrees for 10 to 15 minutes or until the biscuits are light brown. Makes 30 biscuits.

Note: This dough will keep, covered and refrigerated, for up to 1 week.

Delta Salad Dressing

2 garlic cloves, finely chopped
1 tablespoon prepared mustard
1 tablespoon Worcestershire sauce
1/4 cup ketchup
Juice of 1 small grated onion
2 tablespoons water
1/2 tablespoon vinegar
1/4 cup chili sauce
1 cup mayonnaise
1/2 cup vegetable oil
Dash paprika
Dash Tabasco sauce
1 teaspoon pepper

Combine the garlic, mustard, Worcestershire sauce, ketchup, onion juice, water, vinegar, chili sauce, mayonnaise, oil, paprika, Tabasco sauce and pepper in a jar with a tight-fitting lid. Cover the jar and shake until well mixed. Makes about 2 1/2 cups.

Hot Slaw

8 slices bacon
6 green onions, tops and bottoms, chopped
1/3 cup cider vinegar
1 tablespoon brown sugar
1/2 teaspoon salt
4 cups chopped cabbage
1 teaspoon caraway seeds

Fry the bacon in a large skillet until crisp. Drain and crumble. Sauté the green onions in the bacon drippings until tender.

Add the vinegar, brown sugar and salt to the skillet and mix well. Cook until heated through. Add the cabbage and caraway seeds and mix well. Cook, covered, over low heat until the cabbage is tender. Spoon into a serving dish. Top with the crumbled bacon. Makes 4 servings.

Note: This dish goes well with fish.

Red Cabbage Slaw

1/2 head red cabbage
1 1/2 large onions, chopped
1 large green bell pepper, diced
1/2 teaspoon salt
1/4 teaspoon pepper
2 teaspoon sesame seeds
1/4 cup mayonnaise

Grate the cabbage finely. Combine with the onions and bell pepper in a medium bowl and mix well. Add the salt, pepper, sesame seeds and mayonnaise and mix well. Makes 4 to 6 servings.

Sauerkraut Salad

4 cups or 1 (2-pound) can sauerkraut, drained well
1 (16-ounce) can cut green beans, drained
1 cup chopped onion
1/2 cup shredded or chopped carrots
1/4 cup diced green bell pepper
1 1/3 cups sugar
2/3 cup vinegar

Combine the sauerkraut, green beans, onion, carrots and bell pepper in a large bowl and mix well. Combine the sugar and vinegar in a saucepan. Bring to a boil. Pour over the vegetables in the bowl and mix well. Cover and chill. Makes 10 to 12 servings.

Broccoli Salad for a Crowd

- 3/4 pound bacon
- 10 cups fresh broccoli florets
- 2 large red onions, chopped
- 2 cups sliced mushrooms
- 1 cup raisins
- 1 cup walnuts, chopped
- 1 tablespoon sesame seeds (optional)
- 2 cups mayonnaise
- 1/2 cup sugar
- 1/3 cup wine vinegar

Fry the bacon in a skillet until crisp. Drain on paper towels and crumble. Combine the broccoli, onions, mushrooms, raisins, walnuts and sesame seeds in a large bowl and mix well. Add the mayonnaise, sugar and vinegar and mix well. Sprinkle bacon over the top. Makes 20 to 24 servings.

Southwestern Bean and Corn Salad

- 1 (11-ounce) can white Shoe Peg corn, drained
- 1 (15-ounce) can ranch-style black beans, drained
- 1 (8-ounce) jar medium-hot picante sauce
- 2 tablespoons chopped cilantro
- 1 medium white onion, diced
- 1 (15-ounce) can black olives, chopped

Combine the corn, beans, picante sauce, cilantro, onion and olives in a medium bowl and mix well. Serve with chips or crackers. Makes about 6 cups.

Summer Salad Plate

1 head lettuce, torn into bite-size pieces
1 endive, sliced thinly
1 small onion, diced
1/2 green bell pepper, diced
1/2 cup diced celery
4 hard-cooked eggs, diced
Several slices Cheddar cheese, diced or cut into strips
6 radishes, sliced thin
1 carrot, diced
1/2 cup diced ham
1/2 cup diced turkey
1/2 cup cooked flaked fish, chilled
Salad dressing

Combine the lettuce, endive, onion, bell pepper, celery, eggs, Cheddar cheese, radishes, carrot, ham, turkey and fish in a large bowl and mix well. Top with salad dressing of choice and toss to mix well. You may use only turkey or ham or flaked fish if desired. Makes 4 servings.

Baked Beans

1 pound ground beef
2 large onions, chopped
Dash garlic salt
3/4 cup maple-flavored syrup
1 (16-ounce) can pork and beans
1/2 green bell pepper, chopped
3/4 cup sweet tangy barbecue sauce

Crumble the ground beef into a large bowl. Add the onions, garlic salt, syrup, pork and beans, bell pepper and barbecue sauce and mix well. Spoon into a baking dish. Bake, covered, at 350 degrees for 1 1/2 hours.
Makes 4 to 6 servings.

Southern-Style Greens

- $3^1/_2$ to 4 pounds collard, turnip or mustard greens, or a mixture
- $^1/_2$ pound lean salt pork or smoked ham hock
- 1 tablespoon sugar
- 3 beef bouillon cubes
- 8 cups water
- 1 tablespoon margarine
- Salt and pepper to taste

Wash the greens in a sink full of water. Swish the greens to remove any grit. Drain and rinse sink. Repeat washing. Lift the greens out of the water. Remove and discard all large stems. Combine the pork, sugar, bouillon cubes, water and margarine in a large soup pot. Bring to a boil over medium-high heat. Boil for 5 to 10 minutes. Add the greens. Reduce heat and simmer, covered, for $1^1/_2$ hours or until greens are tender. Add salt and pepper to taste. You may peel and quarter turnips and add to the soup pot for the last 30 minutes of cooking. Makes 8 to 10 servings.

Poke Sallet

- 2 gallons poke leaves
- 6 slices bacon
- 6 green onions, sliced
- $^1/_2$ teaspoon sugar
- 1 teaspoon salt
- 1 teaspoon pepper
- 1 teaspoon lemon juice
- 4 hard-cooked eggs, chopped

Gather tender poke leaves when plants are not yet 2 feet high. Cut out any large central veins. Combine poke and water to cover in a large pot. Bring to a boil. Boil for 10 minutes. Drain water. Repeat the process twice. Fry the bacon in a skillet until crisp. Remove from skillet; crumble. Sauté the green onions in the bacon drippings until tender. Add the poke to the skillet along with the sugar, salt, pepper and lemon juice. Simmer for 15 minutes. Top with the eggs and crumbled bacon to serve.
Makes about 4 servings.

Crispy-Coated Eggplant

2 eggplant
1 cup milk
1 egg
1 cup ground Triscuit crackers
1 cup grated Parmesan cheese
$1/3$ cup olive oil

Peel the eggplant and slice into sticks lengthwise. Soak in the milk in a bowl for 10 minutes. Drain and discard milk. Beat the egg in a large bowl. Combine the cracker crumbs and Parmesan cheese on a plate or waxed paper. Dip the eggplant sticks into the egg, then coat with the cracker crumb mixture. Sauté in hot olive oil in a skillet until cooked through. Makes 4 servings.

Eggplant Patties

2 large eggplant
1 pound fresh bulk pork sausage
1 cup finely chopped onion
2 eggs
$1/2$ cup flour
Salt and pepper to taste
1 cup vegetable oil

Peel and chop the eggplant. Combine with water to cover in a large pan. Bring to a boil. Boil about 5 minutes or until tender. Drain. Brown the sausage in a skillet over medium heat, breaking up clumps with a spatula. Drain well. Combine the eggplant, sausage, onion, eggs, flour, salt and pepper in a bowl and mix well. Shape the mixture into small patties. Fry in 375-degree oil in a skillet until brown on both sides, turning once. Makes about 6 servings.

Potato Patties

6 medium potatoes
Salt
1/4 cup (1/2 stick) butter
3 eggs, beaten
2 to 3 cups cracker crumbs
1 1/4 cups (2 1/2 sticks) butter

Peel the potatoes and cut into chunks. Combine with water to cover and salt in a pot. Bring to a boil. Boil until tender. Drain and mash, adding 1/4 cup butter. Mix well. Let stand until cool enough to handle. Form the mixture into small patties. Dip into eggs, then coat with the cracker crumbs. Fry in 1 1/4 cups hot butter in a skillet until golden brown. Makes 18 to 20 patties.

Cheesy Steamed Vegetables

3 potatoes, chopped
2 onions, chopped
1 bunch broccoli, chopped
4 yellow squash, cut into chunks
6 fresh asparagus spears, sliced (optional)
1 (10-ounce) package frozen brussels sprouts
6 carrots, chopped
5 ribs celery, sliced
1 head cauliflower, chopped
2 green bell peppers, chopped
8 ounces mushrooms, sliced
1/4 cup (1/2 stick) margarine
Lawry's seasoned salt to taste
1 (8-ounce) jar Cheez Whiz

Combine the potatoes, onions, broccoli, squash, asparagus, brussels sprouts, carrots, celery, cauliflower, bell peppers and mushrooms in a steamer basket or collapsible vegetable steamer. Place the margarine on top of vegetables and sprinkle them liberally with the seasoned salt. Bring to a boil and steam for 25 minutes or until the carrots are tender. Heat the Cheez Whiz in a microwave or pan of simmering water until it is of a liquid consistency. Serve each 1 cup of vegetables with 2 tablespoons Cheez Whiz. Makes 12 to 15 servings.

Bacony Rutabagas

1 large rutabaga
1 quart water
1 tablespoon sugar
1/2 teaspoon salt
1/2 teaspoon pepper
3 bacon slices
1 teaspoon margarine

Peel the rutabaga and chop it. Combine the water, sugar, salt, pepper, bacon and margarine in a Dutch oven or medium soup pot. Bring to a boil. Add the rutabaga. Cook, covered, for 20 minutes or until the rutabaga is tender. Makes 2 to 4 servings.

Fried Onion Rings

4 large onions
1 cup self-rising flour
Dash salt
2 tablespoons vegetable oil
1 egg white
1/2 cup milk
1/3 cup water
2 cups vegetable oil

Peel the onions and slice 1/4 inch thick. Soak in ice water to cover in a bowl for 30 minutes. Combine the flour, salt, 2 tablespoons vegetable oil, egg white and milk in a large bowl and mix well. Add the water and mix well. Heat 2 cups oil in a soup pot to 375 degrees. Remove the onion slices from water and separate into rings. Dip the rings into the batter, then carefully place in hot oil. Fry in batches until golden brown. Drain on paper towels. Serve hot. Makes 4 to 6 servings.

Cross Fried Onion Rings

1^1/2 cups evaporated milk
3 tablespoons vinegar
4 large onions
1 cup self-rising flour
Dash salt
Dash garlic salt
2 cups vegetable oil

Combine the evaporated milk and vinegar in a medium bowl. Stir until the mixture is thick. Peel the onions and cut into ^{1}/4-inch slices. Separate into rings. Dip the onions into the milk mixture, then coat with a mixture of the flour, salt and garlic salt. Heat oil in a skillet to 375 degrees. Fry onion rings in hot oil in batches until golden brown. Drain on paper towels. Salt again if you like. Serve hot. Makes 4 servings.

Sherried Onions

5 medium onions, sliced
^{1}/2 teaspoon sugar
^{1}/2 teaspoon salt
^{1}/2 teaspoon pepper
^{2}/3 cup (1 stick plus 3 tablespoons) butter
^{1}/2 cup dry sherry or white wine
^{1}/4 cup grated Parmesan cheese

Combine the onions, sugar, salt and pepper in a bowl. Mix gently. Melt the butter in a large heavy skillet over medium heat. Add the onion mixture and cook for 5 to 8 minutes, stirring frequently. Stir in the sherry and cook for 2 to 3 minutes longer. Spoon into a serving dish. Sprinkle with the cheese. Makes 6 servings.

Baked Onions

6 medium onions
6 teaspoons Worcestershire sauce
Lawry's seasoned salt to taste
2 bacon slices, cut into thirds
2 tablespoons margarine

Peel the onions and cut out part of the core. Place each onion on a 6x6-inch square of aluminum foil. Spoon 1 teaspoon Worcestershire sauce into each onion. Sprinkle liberally with seasoned salt. Place a piece of bacon across each open core. Top with 1 teaspoon margarine. Close the foil and crimp to seal. Place the onions in a baking dish or bread pan. Bake at 350 degrees for 45 minutes or grill for 50 minutes. Makes 6 servings.

Cocktail Sauce

1 cup chili sauce
1 cup ketchup
2 tablespoons grated onion
3 tablespoons prepared horseradish
1/2 teaspoon Creole mustard
1 tablespoon lemon juice

Combine the chili sauce, ketchup, onion, horseradish, mustard and lemon juice in a medium bowl and mix well. Chill in the refrigerator until ready to serve. Makes about 2 1/2 cups.

Fruit Sauce for Ham

10 ounces apple jelly
10 ounces pineapple preserves
1 (5-ounce) jar prepared horseradish
1 (6-ounce) jar prepared mustard

Combine the apple jelly, pineapple preserves, horseradish and mustard in a bowl and mix well. Makes about 4 cups.

Mint Sauce for Roast

1/2 cup vinegar
2 tablespoons sugar
1/4 to 1/2 cup fresh mint, chopped

Combine the vinegar and sugar in a bowl. Stir until the sugar dissolves. Add the mint and mix well. Let stand in a warm place until serving time. Add warm water if the vinegar tastes too strong. Serve with roast, cutlets or fish. Makes about 1 cup.

Currant Wine Sauce for Fowl

1 cup currant jelly
1 teaspoon Worcestershire sauce
1 tablespoon prepared horseradish
1 teaspoon dry mustard
1/4 cup lemon juice
1 cup dry red wine

Combine the currant jelly, Worcestershire sauce, horseradish, dry mustard, lemon juice and red wine in a skillet. Heat over low heat until the jelly is melted and the mixture is thickened. Makes about 2 1/2 cups.

Red Red Barbecue Sauce

3/4 cup chopped onion
1/4 cup vegetable oil
1 (8-ounce) can tomato sauce
1 cup ketchup
1/2 cup vinegar
1 teaspoon salt
1/2 teaspoon Tabasco sauce
2 1/2 tablespoons brown sugar
2 tablespoons Worcestershire sauce
3 tablespoons prepared mustard

Sauté the onion in the oil in a saucepan until tender but not brown. Add the tomato sauce, ketchup, vinegar, salt, Tabasco sauce, brown sugar, Worcestershire sauce and mustard. Simmer for 15 minutes. Use to baste meat during cooking. Makes about 4 cups.

Tangy Mustard Barbecue Sauce

1 cup (2 sticks) margarine
1 (6-ounce) jar prepared mustard
1/2 cup ketchup
1/4 teaspoon salt
1 1/2 tablespoons dried onion flakes
Dash pepper
Dash parsley
Dash thyme

Combine the margarine, mustard, ketchup, salt, onion flakes, pepper, parsley and thyme in a saucepan. Heat over low heat until the margarine is melted and the onion is plumped, stirring often. Makes about 3 1/2 cups.

Sausage Gravy

1 pound bulk pork sausage
3 tablespoons self-rising flour
1 small white onion, chopped
Dash garlic salt
Dash Lawry's seasoned salt
2 cups milk

Brown the sausage in a Dutch oven or skillet, stirring until crumbly. Remove the sausage from skillet. Drain all but 3 tablespoons drippings. Add the flour and cook until light brown, stirring constantly. Add the onion to the skillet and sauté until tender. Add the garlic salt, seasoned salt and milk. Add the sausage to the skillet. Cook until thickened, stirring constantly. Add water if the mixture seems too thick. Makes about 4 servings.

Red-Eye Gravy

3 slices country ham
1 tablespoon vegetable oil
1 cup water
1/2 teaspoon cornstarch

Cut slashes in the fat around each ham slice to prevent its curling up during cooking. Brown the ham on both sides in the oil in a large skillet. Add the water. Cook, covered, for 5 minutes. Remove the ham from the liquid. Stir the cornstarch into the cooking liquid. Cook for 3 minutes or until thickened, stirring constantly. Makes 3 servings.

Tomato Gravy

6 bacon slices
3 tablespoons self-rising flour
1 white onion, chopped
4 beef bouillon cubes
1 cup hot water
1 (10-ounce) can diced tomatoes and green chiles
1 (14- to 16-ounce) can whole tomatoes
3 fresh tomatoes, peeled and chopped
1 (8-ounce) can tomato sauce
1 cup water
1 (4-ounce) can mushrooms, drained
1 teaspoon sugar
Salt to taste
Dash red pepper
Dash black pepper
Dash Tabasco sauce

Fry the bacon in a medium skillet. Remove the bacon from the skillet. Stir the flour into the pan drippings. Cook until smooth and thick, stirring constantly. Add the onion and cook until tender. Dissolve the bouillon cubes in 1 cup hot water. Add to the skillet along with the diced tomatoes and green chiles, whole tomatoes, fresh tomatoes, tomato sauce, 1 cup water, mushrooms, sugar, salt, red pepper, black pepper and Tabasco sauce. Crumble the bacon and add to skillet. Simmer until thickened. Serve with biscuits, toast or grits. Makes 6 to 8 servings.

Bread Pudding

- 1/2 cup (1 stick) margarine, softened
- 1 1/2 cups sugar
- 4 eggs
- 1 (5-ounce) can evaporated milk
- 1 1/2 cups water
- 1 teaspoon vanilla extract
- 7 slices white bread

Beat the margarine and sugar in a medium bowl until fluffy. Add the eggs and mix well. Add the evaporated milk, water and vanilla and mix well. Line a 9x13-inch baking pan with bread. Pour the margarine mixture over the bread. Bake at 325 degrees for 1 hour. Makes 6 to 8 servings.

Sinful Banana Pudding

- 1 (6-ounce) package vanilla instant pudding mix
- 2 cups milk
- 1 (14-ounce) can sweetened condensed milk
- 1 tablespoon lemon juice
- 1/2 cup amaretto
- Vanilla extract to taste
- 16 ounces whipped topping
- 3 bananas, sliced
- 1 (8-ounce) package vanilla wafers

Combine the pudding mix, milk and condensed milk in a bowl and mix well. Stir in the lemon juice, amaretto and vanilla. Fold in the whipped topping. Alternate layers of pudding, bananas and vanilla wafers in large bowl. Chill until serving time. Makes 6 servings.

Autumn Persimmon Pudding

$1^1/2$ pounds ripe persimmons
$1^1/2$ cups buttermilk
$1^1/2$ cups sugar
$1^1/4$ cups flour
$^1/2$ teaspoon baking soda
$^1/4$ teaspoon salt
$^1/4$ teaspoon allspice

Combine the persimmons and a small amount of water in a medium saucepan. Bring to a boil over medium heat. Boil until the persimmons turn to mush. Press the pulp through a strainer to remove the skin and seeds. Measure $1^1/2$ cups persimmon pulp. Reserve or freeze the remaining pulp for later use. Combine the persimmon pulp, buttermilk, sugar, flour, baking soda, salt and allspice in a bowl and mix well. Spoon into a greased 2-quart baking dish. Bake at 350 degrees for 20 minutes. Serve with whipped cream. Makes 4 servings.

Butter Pecan Chiffon

1 small package butter pecan instant pudding mix
1 cup milk
8 ounces cream cheese, softened
12 ounces whipped topping
$^1/2$ cup chopped pecans
2 cups small marshmallows

Combine the pudding mix with the milk in a large bowl and mix well. Fold in the cream cheese and whipped topping. Add the pecans and marshmallows. Pour into a serving bowl. Cover and chill. Makes 6 to 8 servings.

Cuban Flan

Sugar
3 large eggs
1/2 teaspoon almond extract
1/2 cup evaporated milk
1 (14-ounce) can sweetened condensed milk
1 tablespoon water

Sprinkle sugar over bottom of metal pudding mold. Cook over high heat until the sugar is caramelized, stirring constantly. Cool to room temperature. Process the eggs, almond extract, evaporated milk, condensed milk and water in a blender on high for 2 minutes. Pour over the sugar in the mold. Place the mold in a pan of water. Bake at 325 degrees for about 25 minutes. Turn off the oven. Let the flan stand in the oven for 2 or more hours. Chill in the refrigerator for 8 hours. Unmold onto a serving plate. Makes 4 to 6 servings.

Southern Rice Custard

3/4 cup uncooked long grain rice
1/2 cup sugar
1 teaspoon (scant) salt
4 cups milk
2 tablespoons butter or margarine, softened

Combine the rice, sugar, salt, milk and butter in a greased 2-quart casserole and mix well. Bake at 300 degrees for 2 1/2 hours. Serve hot or cold. Makes 8 servings.

Apple Cranberry Crisp

- 3 cups chopped peeled green apples
- 1 (12-ounce) package cranberries
- 2 tablespoons flour
- 1 cup sugar
- 1/2 teaspoon cinnamon (optional)
- 1/2 cup packed dark brown sugar
- 1/2 cup flour
- 1/4 teaspoon cinnamon (optional)
- 1/2 cup (1 stick) margarine
- 3/4 cup chopped pecans

Toss the apples and cranberries with a mixture of 2 tablespoons flour, sugar and 1/2 teaspoon cinnamon in a bowl. Spread in a greased 9x13-inch baking dish. Mix the brown sugar, 1/2 cup flour and 1/4 teaspoon cinnamon in a bowl. Cut in the margarine with a pastry cutter or 2 knives until crumbly. Add the pecans. Spoon over the apple mixture. Bake at 325 degrees for 30 to 40 minutes or until the apples are tender and the top is golden brown. Makes 6 servings.

Fried Apple Pies

12 apples, peeled, cored, chopped
3 cups water
1 cup sugar
$1^1/_2$ teaspoons cinnamon
$^1/_2$ teaspoon salt
1 (10-count) can refrigerator biscuits
1 cup flour
2 cups vegetable oil

Combine the apples, water, sugar, cinnamon and salt in a pan. Cook until the apples are tender and falling apart. Separate the biscuits. Place on a floured work surface and roll with a rolling pin to about a 4-inch diameter. Place a saucer over the dough and use it as a guide to trim the dough in a circle. Place 2 tablespoons of apple mixture on one side of each dough circle. Fold the dough over to enclose the filling. Crimp the edges with a fork. Prick the top with a fork. Fry in hot oil in a skillet until golden brown. Makes 10 servings.

Peach Cobbler

$^1/_2$ cup (1 stick) margarine
1 cup sugar
1 cup flour
$^1/_2$ teaspoon salt
1 tablespoon baking powder
$^1/_2$ cup milk
4 cups chopped peeled peaches
$^1/_3$ cup sugar

Melt the margarine in a baking dish in a 375-degree oven. Combine 1 cup sugar, flour, salt and baking powder in a bowl and mix well. Add the milk and mix well. Pour over the hot margarine in the baking dish. Combine the peaches and $^1/_3$ cup sugar in a bowl and mix well. Spoon over the batter. Bake for 45 minutes. Makes 6 to 8 servings.

Old-Fashioned Jam Cake

1 cup sugar
3/4 cup shortening
1/2 cup sour milk
3 eggs
2 cups flour
1 teaspoon baking soda
1 teaspoon cinnamon
1 teaspoon nutmeg
1 teaspoon ground cloves
1 teaspoon allspice
1 cup apricot or pineapple jam

Cream the sugar and shortening in a large bowl until light and fluffy. Add the sour milk and eggs and mix well. Add a mixture of flour, baking soda, cinnamon, nutmeg, cloves and allspice and mix well. Stir in the jam just until blended. Spoon into a greased and floured 9x13-inch cake pan. Bake at 350 degrees for 25 to 30 minutes or until a wooden pick inserted near the center comes out clean. Frost with Cream Cheese Icing (page 183). Makes 15 servings.

Rum Pound Cake

1 cup (2 sticks) butter, softened
3 cups sugar
6 eggs
3 cups flour
1/4 teaspoon baking soda
1 cup sour cream
2 tablespoons rum extract

Cream the butter and sugar in a bowl until light and fluffy. Beat in the eggs 1 at a time. Sift the flour with the baking soda. Add to the creamed mixture alternately with the sour cream and rum extract, mixing well after each addition. Spoon into a greased and floured tube pan. Bake at 350 degrees for 1 hour and 20 minutes. Cool in the pan for 10 minutes; remove to a wire rack to cool completely. Makes 16 servings.

Sweet Potato Cake

2 cups sugar
4 eggs
1 cup vegetable oil
1 teaspoon vanilla extract
2 cups flour
2 teaspoons baking soda
2 teaspoons cinnamon
1 (16-ounce) can sweet potatoes
8 ounces cream cheese, softened
1/2 cup (1 stick) butter or margarine, softened
1 (1-pound) package confectioners' sugar

Combine the sugar and eggs in a bowl and mix well. Mix in the oil and vanilla. Add a mixture of flour, baking soda and cinnamon and mix well. Add the undrained sweet potatoes. Beat for 2 minutes. Spoon into a greased and floured tube pan. Bake at 350 degrees for 1 hour. Combine the cream cheese, butter and confectioners' sugar in a mixing bowl; beat until smooth and creamy. Frost the cake. Makes 8 to 10 servings.

Butter Brickle Cake

1 (29-ounce) can peaches
1 (2-layer) package butter brickle cake mix
1 cup chopped pecans
1 cup shredded coconut
1/2 cup (1 stick) melted margarine

Spread the undrained peaches in an ungreased 9x13-inch cake pan. Sprinkle with the cake mix, pecans and coconut. Drizzle with the margarine. Bake at 350 degrees for 30 to 35 minutes or until light brown. You may bake this cake in a glass baking dish so the peaches can be seen. Makes 15 servings.

Favorite Carrot Cake

2 cups flour
2 teaspoons baking powder
2 teaspoons baking soda
2 tablespoons cinnamon
1 teaspoon salt
2 cups sugar
1 teaspoon vinegar
4 eggs, beaten
1$^{1}/_{2}$ cups vegetable oil
3 cups grated carrots
Cream Cheese Icing
Whole nuts

Combine the flour, baking powder, baking soda, cinnamon and salt in a large bowl and mix well. Add the sugar, vinegar, eggs and oil and mix well. Fold in the carrots. Pour into 3 greased and floured 8-inch cake pans. Bake at 375 degrees for 30 minutes. Let cool on wire racks. Frost with Cream Cheese Icing (below). Arrange the whole nuts on top. Makes 16 servings.

Cream Cheese Icing

$^{1}/_{2}$ cup (1 stick) margarine, softened
8 ounces cream cheese, softened
1 (1-pound) package confectioners' sugar
1 cup chopped pecans

Combine the margarine and cream cheese in a bowl and beat until creamy. Add the confectioners' sugar; beat until of spreading consistency. Stir in the pecans.
Makes 2 to 3 cups.

Choco-Peanut Freezer Dessert

1 (16-ounce) package chocolate sandwich cookies, crushed
1/2 cup (1 stick) melted margarine
2 quarts vanilla ice cream, softened
1 1/2 cups salted Spanish peanuts
2 cups confectioners' sugar
1 1/2 cups evaporated milk
2/3 cup chocolate chips
1/2 cup (1 stick) butter or margarine
1 teaspoon vanilla extract

Combine the cookie crumbs and melted margarine in a bowl and mix well. Press into a 9x13-inch dish. Spread with the ice cream; sprinkle with the peanuts. Freeze until firm. Bring the confectioners' sugar, evaporated milk, chocolate chips and butter to a boil in saucepan. Boil for 8 minutes, stirring constantly. Remove from the heat. Stir in the vanilla. Let stand until cool. Drizzle over frozen layers. Freeze until serving time. Makes 15 servings.

Ice Cream Sandwich Dessert

12 vanilla ice cream sandwiches
1 (12-ounce) jar caramel sauce
8 ounces whipped topping
3 (1 1/4-ounce) toffee bars

Place the ice cream sandwiches in a rectangular baking dish just large enough to hold them in a single layer. Spread most of the caramel sauce over the ice cream bars. Spread the whipped topping over the caramel sauce. Crush the toffee bars and sprinkle over the whipped topping. Drizzle with the remaining caramel sauce and freeze. Cut into squares to serve. Makes 8 to 10 servings.

Praline Graham Yummies

10 to 12 graham crackers, broken into individual rectangles
1/2 cup (1 stick) butter
1/2 cup (1 stick) margarine
1/2 cup sugar
1/2 cup packed brown sugar
1 cup chopped pecans

Arrange the graham crackers in a single layer in an ungreased 10x15-inch baking pan. Bring the butter, margarine, sugar and brown sugar to a boil in a saucepan. Boil for 3 minutes, stirring occasionally. Stir in the pecans. Spread evenly over the graham crackers. Bake at 350 degrees for 10 minutes. Let stand until cool. Break apart. Store in airtight container. Makes 40 servings.

Microwave Pralines

1 (1-pound) package light brown sugar
1 cup whipping cream
2 tablespoons butter or margarine
2 cups pecan halves

Combine the brown sugar and cream in a microwave-safe 3-quart glass bowl and mix well. Microwave on High for 14 minutes, stirring after 7 minutes. Stir in the butter and pecans. Microwave for 1 to 2 minutes or to soft-ball stage. Drop by tablespoonfuls onto waxed paper. Let stand until firm. Makes 20 servings.

Game and Fowl Substitutions

Different varieties of wild game can be substituted within recipes if the meats are of the same type. Use these tables as a guide for substituting in recipes when the game or fowl called for is not available or is out of season.

Game

Type	Item
Fatty	Opossum
	Bear
	Raccoon
Medium	Squirrel
	Rabbit
	Muskrat
	Woodchuck
	Chicken
Lean	Elk
	Moose
	Antelope
	Venison
	Beaver
	Lean beef
	Lean pork

Fowl

Type	Item
Lean, dark meat	Snipe
	Woodcock
	Dove
	Pigeon
	Rabbit
Fatty, dark meat	Duck
	Goose
White meat	Pheasant
	Quail
	Ruffed grouse
	Wild turkey
	Chicken
	Turkey

Nutritional Comparison

The comparison of the compositions of wild game and domestic meats per 100 grams (about 3.6 ounces)

Food and Description	Water (Percent)	Calories	Protein (Percent)	Fat (Percent)
Beef: choice grade, trimmed, raw	51.7	356	16.3	31.6
Pork: composite of trimmed, lean meat, medium fat class, raw	45.5	384	23.6	31.4
Lamb: choice grade, trimmed, raw	64.8	223	17.9	16.0
Beaver: cooked, roasted	56.2	248	29.2	13.7
Raccoon: cooked, roasted	54.8	255	29.2	14.5
Muskrat: cooked, roasted	67.3	153	27.2	4.1
Venison: lean meat, raw	74.0	123	20.6	3.9
Rabbit: raw	59.8	218	29.5	10.1
Chicken: fryers, total edible, raw	53.3	189	23.3	13.0
Duck, Wild: total edible, raw	61.1	233	21.1	15.8
Pheasant: total edible, raw	72.8	133	23.6	3.6
Quail: total edible, raw	70.0	134	21.8	4.5
Bass, Largemouth: raw	60.8	196	21.5	8.5
Catfish: raw	78.0	103	17.6	3.1
Frogs' legs	81.9	73	16.4	0.3
Crawfish	82.5	72	14.6	0.5

Source: Alabama Cooperative Extension Service at Auburn University

Equivalent Chart

When the Recipe Calls for	Use
Baking	
1/2 cup butter	4 ounces
2 cups butter	1 pound
4 cups all-purpose flour	1 pound
4 1/2 to 5 cups sifted cake flour	1 pound
1 square chocolate	1 ounce
1 cup semisweet chocolate chips	6 ounces
4 cups marshmallows	1 pound
2 1/4 cups packed brown sugar	1 pound
4 cups confectioners' sugar	1 pound
2 cups granulated sugar	1 pound
Cereal/Bread	
1 cup fine dry bread crumbs	4 to 5 slices
1 cup soft bread crumbs	2 slices
1 cup small bread cubes	2 slices
1 cup fine cracker crumbs	25 saltines
1 cup fine graham cracker crumbs	15 graham crackers
1 cup vanilla wafer crumbs	22 wafers
1 cup crushed cornflakes	3 cups, uncrushed
4 cups cooked macaroni	8 ounces, uncooked
3 1/2 cups cooked rice	1 cup, uncooked
Dairy	
1 cup shredded cheese	4 ounces
1 cup cottage cheese	8 ounces
1 cup sour cream	8 ounces
1 cup whipped cream	1/2 cup heavy cream
2/3 cup evaporated milk	1 small can
1 2/3 cups evaporated milk	1 (13-ounce) can
Fruit	
4 cups sliced or chopped apples	4 medium
1 cup mashed bananas	3 medium
2 cups pitted cherries	4 cups, unpitted
2 1/2 cups shredded coconut	8 ounces
4 cups cranberries	1 pound
1 cup pitted dates	1 (8-ounce) package
1 cup candied fruit	1 (8-ounce) package
3 to 4 tablespoons lemon juice plus 1 tablespoon grated lemon rind	1 lemon
1/3 cup orange juice plus 2 teaspoons grated orange rind	1 orange
4 cups sliced peaches	8 medium
2 cups pitted prunes	1 (12-ounce) package
3 cups raisins	1 (15-ounce) package

Equivalent Chart

When the Recipe Calls for	Use
Meats	
4 cups chopped cooked chicken	1 (5-pound) chicken
3 cups chopped cooked meat	1 pound, cooked
2 cups cooked ground meat	1 pound, cooked
Nuts	
1 cup chopped nuts	4 ounces, shelled 1 pound, unshelled
Vegetables	
2 cups cooked green beans	1/2 pound fresh or 1 (16-ounce) can
2 1/2 cups lima beans or red beans	1 cup dried, cooked
4 cups shredded cabbage	1 pound
1 cup grated carrot	1 large
8 ounces fresh mushrooms	1 (4-ounce) can
1 cup chopped onion	1 large
4 cups sliced or chopped potatoes	4 medium
2 cups canned tomatoes	1 (16-ounce) can

Metric Equivalents

Liquid

1 teaspoon = 5 milliliters
1 tablespoon = 15 milliliters
1 fluid ounce = 30 milliliters
1 cup = 250 milliliters
1 pint = 500 milliliters

Dry

1 quart = 1 liter
1 ounce = 30 grams
1 pound = 450 grams
2.2 pounds = 1 kilogram

Measurement Equivalents

1 tablespoon = 3 teaspoons
2 tablespoons = 1 ounce
4 tablespoons = 1/4 cup
5 1/3 tablespoons = 1/3 cup
8 tablespoons = 1/2 cup
12 tablespoons = 3/4 cup
16 tablespoons = 1 cup
1 cup = 8 ounces or 1/2 pint
4 cups = 1 quart
4 quarts = 1 gallon

1 (6 1/2- to 8-ounce) can = 1 cup
1 (10 1/2- to 12-ounce) can = 1 1/4 cups
1 (14- to 16-ounce) can = 1 3/4 cups
1 (16- to 17-ounce) can = 2 cups
1 (18- to 20-ounce) can = 2 1/2 cups
1 (29-ounce) can = 3 1/2 cups
1 (46- to 51-ounce) can = 5 3/4 cups
1 (6 1/2- to 7 1/2-pound) can or
Number 10 = 12 to 13 cups

Basic Substitutions

When the Recipe Calls for	You can Substitute:
Flour	
1 cup sifted all-purpose flour	1 cup minus 2 tablespoons unsifted all-purpose flour
1 cup sifted cake flour	1 cup minus 2 tablespoons sifted all-purpose flour
1 cup sifted self-rising flour	1 cup sifted all-purpose flour plus $1\frac{1}{2}$ teaspoons baking powder and a pinch of salt
Milk/Cream	
1 cup buttermilk	1 cup plain yogurt, or 1 tablespoon lemon juice or vinegar plus enough milk to measure 1 cup—let stand for 5 minutes before using
1 cup whipping cream or half-and-half	$\frac{7}{8}$ cup whole milk plus $1\frac{1}{2}$ tablespoons butter
1 cup light cream	$\frac{7}{8}$ cup whole milk plus 3 tablespoons butter
1 cup sour cream	1 cup plain yogurt
1 cup sour milk	1 cup plain yogurt
1 cup whole milk	1 cup skim or nonfat milk plus 2 tablespoons butter or margarine
Seasonings	
1 teaspoon allspice	$\frac{1}{2}$ teaspoon cinnamon plus $\frac{1}{8}$ teaspoon cloves
1 cup ketchup	1 cup tomato sauce plus $\frac{1}{2}$ cup sugar plus 2 tablespoons vinegar
1 teaspoon Italian spice	$\frac{1}{4}$ teaspoon each oregano, basil, thyme, rosemary plus dash of cayenne
1 teaspoon lemon juice	$\frac{1}{2}$ teaspoon vinegar
Sugar	
1 cup confectioners' sugar	$\frac{1}{2}$ cup plus 1 tablespoon granulated sugar
1 cup granulated sugar	$1\frac{3}{4}$ cups confectioners' sugar, 1 cup packed light brown sugar or $\frac{3}{4}$ cup honey
Other	
1 package active dry yeast	$\frac{1}{2}$ cake compressed yeast
1 teaspoon double-acting baking powder	$\frac{1}{4}$ teaspoon cream of tartar plus $\frac{1}{4}$ teaspoon baking soda
1 cup dry bread crumbs	$\frac{3}{4}$ cup cracker crumbs or 1 cup cornflake crumbs
1 cup butter	$\frac{7}{8}$ cup vegetable oil or 1 cup margarine
1 tablespoon cornstarch	2 tablespoons all-purpose flour
1 cup dark corn syrup	$\frac{3}{4}$ cup light corn syrup plus $\frac{1}{4}$ cup light molasses
1 cup light corn syrup	1 cup maple syrup
$1\frac{2}{3}$ ounces semisweet chocolate	1 ounce unsweetened chocolate plus 4 teaspoons granulated sugar
1 ounce unsweetened chocolate	3 tablespoons unsweetened baking cocoa plus 1 tablespoon butter or margarine
1 (1-ounce) square chocolate	$\frac{1}{4}$ cup baking cocoa plus 1 teaspoon shortening
1 cup honey	1 to $1\frac{1}{4}$ cups sugar plus $\frac{1}{4}$ cup liquid or 1 cup corn syrup or molasses
Currants	Raisins
1 egg	$\frac{1}{4}$ cup mayonnaise

Vegetable Saucery

Basic White Sauce

Ingredients	Thin	Medium	Thick
Margarine	2 tablespoons	1/4 cup	6 tablespoons
Flour	2 tablespoons	1/4 cup	6 tablespoons
Milk	2 cups	2 cups	2 cups
Salt	1 teaspoon	1 teaspoon	1 teaspoon

Melt margarine in a saucepan over low heat. Stir in the flour until smooth. Add the milk gradually, stirring constantly. Cook over medium heat until bubbly, stirring constantly. Season with salt. Add pepper to taste.

- Substitute 1 cup chicken broth for 1 cup milk if preferred.
- Substitute evaporated skim milk for whole milk to make Low-Calorie Basic White Sauce.

Variations

Sauce	Add to basic sauce	Use with
Cheese	1/2 cup sharp Cheddar cheese 2 drops of Worcestershire sauce	broccoli, brussels sprouts, cabbage, cauliflower
Curry	2 to 3 teaspoons curry powder 1/8 teaspoon ginger	asparagus, carrots, mushrooms, squash
Dill	1 to 2 teaspoons dillweed	cauliflower, green beans
Mushroom	1/2 cup sautéed mushrooms	broccoli, peas, spinach
Mustard	1 to 2 tablespoons prepared mustard or Dijon mustard	bok choy, green beans, onions, tomatoes
Parsley	2 tablespoons chopped parsley	peas, potatoes
Tomato	1/4 cup chili sauce Dash of Tabasco sauce	eggplant, onions, peppers, zucchini

Wine Guide

The pairing of good food with fine wine is one of the great pleasures of life. The rule that you drink white wine only with fish and fowl and red wine with meat no longer applies—just let your own taste and personal preference be the guide. Remember to serve light wines with lighter foods and full-bodied wines with rich foods so the food and wine will complement rather than overpower each other.

The best wine to cook with is the one you will be serving at the table. The real secret is to cook with a good wine, as the alcohol evaporates during the cooking process, leaving only the actual flavor of the wine. A fine wine with rich body and aroma will insure a distinct and delicate flavor. When used in cooking, the wine should accent and enhance the natural flavor of the food while adding its own inviting fragrance and flavor.

Semidry White Wines

These wines have a fresh fruity taste and are best served young.
Serve with dove, quail, or shellfish in cream sauce; roast turkey, duck, or goose; seafood, pasta, or salad; fish in an herbed butter sauce.

* Johannisberg Riesling – (Yo-hann-is-burg Rees-ling) * Frascati – (Fras-kah-tee)
* Gewürztraminer – (Guh-vurts-trah-mee-ner) * Bernkasteler – (Barn-kahst-ler)
* Sylvaner Riesling – (Sihl-van-uhr Rees-ling) * Fendant – (Fahn-dawn)
* Dienheimer – (Deen-heim-er) * Kreuznach – (Kroytz-nock)

Dry White Wines

These wines have a crisp, refreshing taste and are best served young.
Serve with chicken, turkey, and cold meat; roast young gamebirds and waterfowl; shellfish; fried or grilled fish; ham and veal.

* Vouvray – (Voo-vray) * Chablis – (Sha-blee) * Chardonnay – (Shar-doh-nay)
* Pinot Blanc – (Pee-noh Blahn) * Chenin Blanc – (Shen-ihn Blahn)
* Pouilly-Fuissé – (Poo-yee Fwee-say) * Orvieto Secco – (Ohr-vyay-toh Say-koh)
* Piesporter Trocken – (Peez-porter Trawk-uhn) * Meursault – (Mehr-soh)
* Hermitage Blanc – (Ehr-mee-tahzh Blahn) * Pinot Grigio – (Pee-noh Gree-jo)
* Verdicchio – (Vehr-deek-kyoh) * Sancerre – (Sahn-sehr)
* Sauvignon Blanc – (Soh-vihn-yohn Blahn) * Soave – (So-ah-veh)

Light Red Wines

These wines have a light taste and are best served young.
Serve with grilled chicken; fowl with highly seasoned stuffings; soups and stews; Creole foods; veal or lamb.

* Beaujolais – (Boh-zhuh-lay) * Bardolino – (Bar-doh-lee-noh)
* Valpolicella – (Vahl-paw-lee-chehl-lah)
* Moulin-à-Vent Beaujolais – (Moo-lan-nah-vahn Boh-zhuh-lay)
* Barbera – (Bar-beh-rah) * Lambrusco – (Lam-broos-koh)
Lirac – (Lee-rak)
* Nuits-Saint-Georges "Villages" – (Nwee San Zhawrzh)
* Gamay Beaujolais – (Ga-may Boh-zhuh-lay)
* Santa Maddalena – (Sahn-tah Mahd-dah-leh-nah)
* Merlot del Ticino – (Mehr-loh dehl Tee-chee-noh)

Hearty Red Wines

These wines have a heavier taste, improve with age, and are best opened thirty minutes before serving. Serve with game including duck, goose, venison, and hare; pot roast; red meats including beef, lamb, and veal; hearty foods; cheese and egg dishes, pastas, and highly seasoned foods.

* Barbaresco – (Bar-bah-ress-koh) * Barolo – (Bah-roh-loh)
* Burgundy – (Ber-gun-dee) * Zinfandel – (Zihn-fuhn-dehl)
* Chianti Riserva – (Kee-ahn-tee Ree-zehr-vah) * Bordeaux – (Bohr-doh)
* Côte-Rotie – (Koht Roh-tee) * Hermitage – (Ehr-mee-tahzh)
* Taurasi – (Tow-rah-zee) * Merlot – (Mehr-loh)
* Syrah – (See-rah) * Châteauneuf-du-Pape – (Shah-toh-nuhf-doo-Pahp)
* Petite Sirah – (Peh-teet Sih-rah) * Côte de Beaune – (Koht duh Bohn)
* Cabernet Sauvignon – (Ka-behr-nay Soh-vihn-yohn)

Index

Cooking Wild Game & Fish
Southern Style

P.O. Box 12303
Jackson, Mississippi 39236

Please send _______ copies of *Cooking Wild Game & Fish Southern Style*
@ $19.95 each $ ______________

Mississippi residents add $1.40 sales tax per book $ ______________

Postage and handling @ $1.50 each $ ______________

Total $ ______________

Name ______________________________

Address ______________________________

City ______________ State ______ Zip ______

Method of Payment: [ ] MasterCard [ ] VISA [ ] Discover [ ] American Express
[ ] Check payable to Cooking Wild Game & Fish Southern Style

Account Number ______________ Expiration Date ______

Signature ______________________________

Photocopies will be accepted.